MW01628104

The Botanical Ark

text by Alan & Susan Carle
photography by Norbert Guthier

Mission Statement

The MISSION STATEMENT of The Botanical Ark is:

To actively participate in global rainforest conservation

...by developing and demonstrating a greater understanding of the link between tropical peoples and their plants,

...by emphasising the uses and values that indigenous cultures from around the world place upon their plants,

...by illustrating how valuable and essential rainforest plants have become in our lives,

...by providing educational opportunities, appreciation of the biodiversity, wealth and potential of tropical forest ecosystems,

...by offering opportunities for people to help save some of the world's rainforest and the peoples who inhabit them.

Das HAUPTANLIEGEN der Botanical Ark ist:

Aktive Teilnahme am weltweiten Schutz des Regenwaldes

...durch das Entwickeln und Aufzeigen eines tieferen Verständnisses der Verbindung zwischen der tropischen Bevölkerung und ihren Pflanzen,

...durch die Betonung des Nutzens und der Werte, die einheimische Kulturen auf der ganzen Welt aus ihren Pflanzen schöpfen,

...durch das Aufzeigen, wie wertvoll und wesentlich Regenwaldpflanzen auch für unser Leben geworden sind,

...durch die Schaffung von Ausbidungsmöglichkeiten, die die Wertschätzung der biologischen Vielfalt, die Reichhaltigkeit und das Potential der tropischer Wälder vermitteln,

...durch das Aufzeigen von Möglichkeiten, wie Menschen helfen können, einige der Regenwälder dieser Welt und deren einheimische Bewohner zu retten.

Preface

Tropical moist forests are the richest in biological diversity -- owing to the sheer number and variety of plants, animals, fungi, and micro-organisms -- of all the biological communities on Earth. Occupying no more than 5 percent of the world's land surface, these forests are home to well over half of the total number of organisms that share our planet with us. Of all of these forests, the most unusual, the ones with the highest proportion of strange, relictual and unique organisms, are those of Australia -- the home of the authors of this book.

As the total human population has exploded from 2.5 billion in 1950 to over 6 billion today -- including an increase of 50 percent during the last 25 years alone -- and as our standards of living and expectations have continued to rise, environments have been, and are continuing to be, destroyed throughout the world. The character of the atmosphere has been changed; soils and agricultural lands have been devastated, losing a great deal of their fertility and much of their resilience; and the extinction of biological diversity has been accelerated far beyond historical levels. Only fragments of tropical moist forests are likely to remain when the human population of the world. We hope this occurs sometime during the next several decades, perhaps during our grandchildren's lifetime. Despite ample demonstrations of the usefulness of tropical forest products for people, we know very little about these forests -- perhaps one twentieth of the species have been discovered -- and yet we are destroying them with growing speed.

It all sounds very impersonal and not like something we can deal with ourselves. Yet the Carles, with impressive dedication, have done just that, and done it magnificently! This book is a celebration of their realisation, based on extensive travels through the tropics, that the destruction of the forests represents a truly important problem for all of us. Their highly successful efforts to create a unique botanical garden, or botanical ark, in the northeastern corner of Australia, will help to save, understand, and appreciate the wonderful beauty of the rain forests. Their appreciation of indigenous cultures, which they celebrate as part of the unique ecosystems, is a necessary ingredient in saving the whole of nature. Using their garden and their resources to raise awareness of tropical forests, they have demonstrated an unavoidable truth -- that each of us has a choice, and that each can make a difference.

Dr. Peter H. Raven

The important question is not one of whether the world will be saved or lost -- it is what kind of a world we shall choose to pass on to the generations that come after us. More than two centuries of the Industrial Revolution have made the world a much less interesting and beautiful place than it was a few centuries ago. We will not succeed in slowing these trends by wishing for miraculous solutions, but we can slow them by dealing with them individually, as consumers, as visitors, as political beings -- in short, by doing something about it! As the Carles have shown so clearly, we do have a choice. Enjoy this lovely book, illustrated with Norbert Guthier's marvelous photographs, and resolve to make a difference yourself!

Dr. Peter H. Raven,
Director, Missouri Botanical Garden

Den üppigsten Artenreichtum der Erde findet man in den tropischen Regenwäldern - eine ungeheure Menge und Vielfalt an Pflanzen, Tieren, Pilzen und Mikroorganismen aus allen Bereichen der biologischen Gemeinschaften. Obwohl sie nur etwa 5 % der Landfläche der Erde bedecken, beherbergen die Regenwälder weit über die Hälfte aller Organismen, mit denen wir uns den Lebensraum auf der Erde teilen. Die ungewöhnlichsten dieser Wäldern, die mit dem größten Anteil überraschender, urweltlicher und einzigartiger Organismen, sind die in Australien - der Heimat der Autoren dieses Buches.

Mit der explosionsartigen Zunahme der Weltbevölkerung von 2,5 Milliarden im Jahre 1950 auf über 6 Milliarden heute - bei einer Zunahme von rund 50 Prozent allein in den letzten 25 Jahren - und dem Anstieg unseres Lebensstandards und der Lebenserwartung wurde und wird die Umwelt auch heute noch weltweit zerstört. Die Zusammensetzung der Atmosphäre hat sich bereits verändert, Böden und Ackerland haben einen Großteil ihrer Fruchtbarkeit und Fähigkeit zur Erneuerung verloren, und das Artensterben hat sich weit über jedes bisherige Maß hinaus beschleunigt. Nur noch winzige Teile des tropischen Regenwaldes werden existieren, wenn sich das Bevölkerungswachstum in einigen Jahrzehnten hoffentlich auf einem stabilen Level eingependelt hat - vielleicht erst während der Lebenszeit unserer Enkelkinder.

Trotz wiederholter Darlegungen der Nützlichkeit von Produkten aus tropischen Regenwäldern, wissen wir noch immer sehr wenig über diese Urwälder - vielleicht nur ein zwanzigstel der Arten gelten bis heute als entdeckt - und dennoch zerstören wir die Wälder mit zunehmender Geschwindigkeit. Das klingt alles sehr abstrakt und so, als könnten wir persönlich nichts dagegen tun. Aber die Familie Carle hat, mit beeindruckender Hingabe, genau dies versucht. Mit gross-artigem Erfolg! Dieses Buch widmet sich ihre Erkenntnis, die sie auf vielen Reisen durch die Tropen bestätigt fanden, dass die Zerstörung dieser Wälder ein wirklich wichtiges Problem ist, das uns alle angeht.

Ihre inzwischen sehr erfolgreichen Anstrengungen, einen einzigartigen botanischen Garten, die "Botanical Ark"(botanische Arche), im Nordosten Australiens zu schaffen, werden helfen, die wunderbare Schönheit der Regenwälder zu retten, zu verstehen und wertzuschätzen. Ihre Berücksichtigung einheimischer Kulturen, welche sie als Teil der einzigartigen Ökosysteme verstehen, ist ein notwendiger Bestandteil für die Rettung der Natur. Indem sie ihren Garten und all ihre Möglichkeiten einsetzen, um das Bewusstsein für die tropischen Wälder zu wecken, haben sie unwiderlegbar bewiesen, dass jeder von uns die Wahl hat und auch der einzelne etwas bewirken kann.

Die entscheidende Frage ist nicht, ob die Welt gerettet wird oder nicht - sondern eher, wie die Welt aussehen soll, die wir an zukünftige Generationen weitergeben möchten. Gut zweihundert Jahre industrielle Revolution haben unsere Welt zu einem viel weniger interessanten, beziehungsweise weniger schönen Ort werden lassen, als er es noch wenige hundert Jahre zuvor war. Wir werden diesen Trend nicht erfolgreich verlangsamen, indem wir auf Wunder hoffen. Aber wir können etwas erreichen, wenn jeder einzelne handelt, als Verbraucher, als Besucher oder als politisch Aktiver - kurz, wenn sich jeder dafür einsetzt! Wie uns die Familie Carle so klar gezeigt hat, haben wir die Wahl. Geniessen Sie das wunderschöne Buch, illustriert mit Norbert Guthiers fantastischen Aufnahmen und entscheiden Sie sich dafür, auch selbst etwas zu tun!

Dr. Peter H. Raven
Direktor, Missouri Botanical Garden

Australia

Imagine a land called 'Oz', where grains of sand can tell a history 3,500,000,000 years old. Where the grasshoppers stand 2 m (6') tall and are sometimes called kangaroos.Where the red centre glows at each sunrise and sunset and whose warmth and spirit trickle to its distant shores.

Imagine a human history so ancient that all the history books will have to be rewritten, a place where the local inhabitants crossed oceans more than 30,000 years before the Phoenicians sailed the Mediterranean.

Imagine plants and animals so different that more than 80% occur nowhere else on earth.

Imagine the driest continent on earth, that stretches endlessly, ravaged by droughts, wildfires and periodically severe floods.

The indigenous Koala

Stellen Sie sich ein Land vor, ein Traumland, das wir "Oz" nennen wollen. Sandkörner erzählen dort von ihrer 3,5 Milliarden Jahre alten Geschichte und Grashüpfer sind stattliche 2 m groß; man nennt sie Kängurus. Bei Tagesanbruch erscheint ein Feuerball aus der Mitte des Sonnensystems glutrot am Horizont dieses Traumlandes und verströmt seine lebenspendende Energie bis in die entlegendsten Winkel der weitläufigen Küsten.

Stellen Sie sich eine Menschheitsgeschichte vor, die so weit zurück reicht, dass alle vorhandenen Geschichtsbücher neu geschrieben werden müssen, und Ureinwohner, die Weltmeere überquerten, schon 30.000 Jahre bevor die Phönizier über das Mittelmeer segelten.

Stellen Sie sich Pflanzen und Tiere vor, die so andersartig sind, dass 80 % davon nirgendwo sonst auf der Erde vorkommen.

Stellen Sie sich "Oz" als Teil des trockensten Kontinents der Erde vor, unendlich weit, geplagt von Dürre, Buschfeuern aber auch periodischen, schweren Überschwemmungen.

Ellis Beach / Cairns in the early morning

Queensland

Queensland epitomises this land called 'Oz'. It mirrors much of the continent, with its vastness, dryness, and uniqueness.

The Great Barrier Reef hugs the east coast for 2,500 km (1500 miles) and the great dividing range lies just inland from the north to the south. To the west one encounters the dry lands and the deserts, and to the usually dry northwest the channel country turns into an inland sea once every blue moon (during the monsoons).

There are places where it can take 10 years for the rains to come. And places where so many different dinosaurs lie dormant amongst the rocky outcrops. Their story is of a very different, but equally unique era.

Aborigines lived on this land for more than 30,000 years and practiced land management techniques which modified the landscape for ease of hunting and travelling. They established trade routes and cultural events. Evidence of their closeness to the land is found in aboriginal middens, in some of the richest rock art found on earth, and in their oral history, as told from the dream-time.

Dieses Traumland gibt es wirklich: Queensland im Nordosten Australiens. Mit seiner unendlichen Weite, Trockenheit und Einzigartigkeit spiegelt es den gesamten Kontinent wieder.

Das Great Barrier Reef umschließt die Ostküste auf einer Länge von 2.500 km und auch der küstennahe Gebirgszug Great Dividing Range folgt der Nord-Süd-Ausrichtung. Westlich davon findet man die trockenen Gebiete und Wüsten, im Nordwesten dagegen verwandelt sich das normalerweise trockene Flachland während des Monsuns hin und wieder in einen Binnensee.

Es gibt Landstriche, wo für 10 Jahre kein Tropfen Regen fällt und Gegenden, wo zwischen Felsvorsprüngen die Überreste der verschiedensten Dinosaurierarten schlummern. Ihre Geschichte erzählt von einer ganz andereren aber ebenso einzigartigen Ära.

Aborigines leben hier seit über 30.000 Jahren. Sie veränderten die Landschaft, um das Jagen und Reisen zu vereinfachen. Sie legten Handelsrouten an und führten kulturelle Veranstaltungen durch. Beweise für ihre Verbundenheit mit dem Land findet man in den "Aboriginal Middens", die zu den prächtigsten Felsmalereien der Welt gehören, und in ihrer mündlich überlieferten Geschichte, die noch heute von der »Traumzeit« berichtet.

The Heart Reef / Whitsunday Ilands

Ellis Beach / Cairns

The Tropical North

Try to imagine that a small part of this great land is always wet and green.

In the northeast of Queensland where the mountains reach their highest peaks and come closest to the coast, we encounter 'The Wet Tropics'. Rainfall varies from 1000mm (40")per year to more than 12,000mm (480") on the highest peaks, making this area one of the wettest in the world.

The climate is tropical, yet mild. The Coral Sea spawns warm moist winds that moderate the heat yet sometimes turn (violent) on us.

Nur ein ganz kleiner Teil dieses großen Landes ist immer feucht und grün: "the wet tropics".

Sie liegen im Nordwesten von Queensland, wo die Berge am höchsten sind und bis dicht an die Küste reichen. Der Niederschlag schwankt zwischen 1.000 mm bis zu Spitzenwerten von mehr als 12.000 mm pro Jahr. Damit zählt diese Gegend zu den feuchtesten der Welt.

Das Klima ist tropisch aber mild. Von der Coral Sea kommen warme, feuchte Winde. Sie mildern die Hitze, können sich aber gelegentlich auch zu heftigen Tropenstürmen entwickeln.

Barren Gorge near Cairns

The coastline of Port Douglas

Early white pioneers searched the wet tropical forests to fell the giant red cedars, and settlers then cleared the coastal plains to plant sugar cane and other crops. Gold was discovered in the ranges and towns and cities developed along the coast.

The wet tropics would never be the same. Agriculture expanded, more forests were chopped down, and for a time there seemed no end to bigger dreams and more wealth.

History was made just north of The Botanical Ark, where in 1983-84 a group of dedicated conservationists tried to stop a new road from being pushed through the rain forest. The road was established, but the conservationists brought to the nation's and world's attention the uniqueness of this precious resource.

World Heritage listing was proclaimed over much of the remaining rain forests.

Frühe weiße Siedler durchforsteten die feuchten Tropenwälder nach riesigen roten Zedern - und fällten sie. Dann rodeten sie die flachen, küstennahen Gebiete, um Zuckerrohr und andere Feldfrüchte anzubauen. Gold wurde entdeckt und entlang der Küste entstanden Dörfer und Städte.

Das war das Ende dieser tropischen Region in ihrer bisherigen Form. Der Ackerbau dehnte sich aus, weiterer Urwald wurde gerodet. Für einige Zeit schienen die Möglichkeiten für noch größere Träume und weiter wachsenden Wohlstand grenzenlos.

Geschichte wurde etwas nördlich der "Botanical Ark" 1983-84 von Umweltschützern geschrieben. Sie versuchten, den Bau einer neuen Straße durch den Regenwald zu verhindern. Zwar wurde die Straße am Ende doch gebaut, aber die Aktionen der Umweltschützer lenkten die nationale und internationale Aufmerksamkeit auf die einzigartigen und wertvollen Naturschätze dieser Gegend.

Weite Teile des verbliebenen Regenwaldes wurden zum Weltkulturerbe erklärt.

Daintree National Park

Licuala fan palms / Daintree National park

Land Philosophy

We (Individuals) can never really own land. Human life is limited generally by biological considerations, and given normal life spans we cannot expect to inhabit land forever.

The right to occupy land entails some responsibilities - and we feel that it is our responsibility to hand it over to the next generation in better shape than when we commenced occupation. If every land occupier accepted this as an obligation then the health of the planet would improve quite rapidly.

It is an unfortunate fact that many humans exploit the land for profit without considering its long-term vitality. In the process they often destroy or damage its sustainable wealth.

Land occupation should be conditional to maintaining and better yet, improving its sustainable wealth. What we need are governments willing to re-define our attitude towards land by legislating for these changes on all titles, and insuring that titles will not be sold or transferred until these requirements are met and the potential recipient illustrates an understanding of his or her obligations for the future.

Who decides what is better or worse? Let nature decide - Water, air and soil quality can be measured, and so can biodiversity. These are the criteria we need to embrace.

We purchased the land on which The Botanical Ark grows from cattle farmers, who acquired it from sugar cane growers. We are planting a blanket of vegetation to protect the soils from erosion, to provide a carbon sink and clean air to breathe. The wildlife is returning. These are encouraging signs.

Unserer Meinung nach können Menschen Land nicht wirklich besitzen. Schon gar nicht auf Dauer, ist doch unsere Lebenserwartung aus biologischen Gründen begrenzt. So bleibt uns nur die Landnutzung.

Land zu nutzen, beinhaltet Rechte aber auch Pflichten. Wir finden, dass es unsere Pflicht ist, Land, das wir für uns nutzen, in einer besseren Verfassung an die nächste Generation weiterzugeben, als wie es bei der Übernahme war. Würde jeder Landbenutzer so verfahren, würde sich unser Planet sehr schnell erholen.

Es ist eine unglückselige Tatsache, dass viele Menschen das Land ausbeuten, ohne die Langzeitwirkungen zu bedenken. Dabei zerstören sie oft nachhaltig die nährenden Eigenschaften des Bodens.

Landbesitz sollte vom Erhalt, oder besser noch, von der Verbesserung der Bodenqualität abhängig gemacht werden. Was wir brauchen sind Regierungen, die willens sind, unsere Einstellung gegenüber Grund und Boden neu zu definieren. Besitzurkunden sollten eine gesetzliche Regelung zur Bodenschonung enthalten. Der Verkauf bzw. die Weitergabe von Land kann dann nur beurkundet werden, wenn diese Schutzauflagen erfüllt werden. Der potentzielle Nachfolger seinerseits muss ein klares Verständnis für seine zukünftigen Verpflichtungen nachweisen.

Wer bestimmt, was besser oder schlechter ist? Lassen wir die Natur selbst entscheiden: Die Qualität von Wasser, Luft und Boden kann gemessen werden, ebenso die Artenvielfalt. Das sind die Maßstäbe, die zählen sollten.

Wir erwarben das Land, auf dem sich heute die "Botanical Ark" befindet, von Viehbauern; die wiederum hatten es von Zuckerrohranbauern übernommen. Wir pflanzten Bodendecker an, um Bodenerosion zu verhindern, und reinere Luft zu haben. Die ursprüngliche Natur kommt zurück. Das ist ein ermutigendes Zeichen.

Elinjaa Falls / The Tablelands

Finding our home

Our search for the most suitable block of land to raise our family on had to meet a few criteria that many people seem to overlook. They were: clean air to breathe, pure fresh water to drink, suitable land to grow crops free from harmful poisons, and an environment free from crime.

We also wanted to be in the most tropical part of Australia. For us that meant it had to be the warmest and wettest part of North Queensland. For a few years we searched up and down the coast from Cairns, the unofficial 'capital' of Tropical Queensland. We had lived in Kuranda, a hamlet in the rainforest ranges to the west, but found it just a little too cool for our 'tropical paradise'. We had lived in Gordonvale, just to the South, but found it too 'windy'. We understood that if we keep to the coast and head north, where the mountains get close to the sea, that it would get warmer and wetter- so north we searched. Cape York Peninsula is an exciting wilderness but a bit too dry and isolated. Opportunities for schooling and work were limited, hospitals too far away and transportation of any goods was a real challenge.

The Douglas Shire appealed to us most. The drive north from Cairns passes some of the most beautiful coastal scenery in the country. Clean, people-less beaches and forested mountains hug the coast. The picture perfect postcard views of the coastal road make way for sugar fields with rainforest mountain backdrops, where green turns to darker shades of blue as the wilderness blends into the never-never. The sugar industry finishes here and the cane fields make way for rich cattle fattening farms along the Daintree Valley. Further north (across the Daintree river) the farms get smaller and the dense rainforest meets the sea. For the present - and the most part - nature has retained its dominance.

Das Stück Land, das für die besonderen Pläne unserer Familie geeignet war, musste einige Kriterien erfüllen, die viele Menschen scheinbar übersehen. Diese waren: saubere Luft zum Atmen, reines Wasser zum Trinken, Grund und Boden, auf dem man Früchte frei von Giftstoffen anbauen kann, und eine Umgebung ohne Kriminalität.

Außerdem wollten wir im tropischsten Teil Australiens leben. So kam für uns nur die wärmste und feuchteste Gegend von North Queensland in Frage. Für einige Jahre suchten wir ober- und unterhalb der Küste von Cairns, der inoffiziellen Hauptstadt des tropischen Queensland. Wir lebten in Kuranda, einer Siedlung im westlich gelegenen Regenwald. Aber wir fanden es dort etwas zu kühl für unser "tropisches Paradies". Dann lebten wir etwas südlich davon in Gordonvale. Dort war es uns zu windig. Als wir herausfanden, dass es weiter nördlich, wo die Berge bis ans Meer reichen, zunehmend wärmer und feuchter wird, suchten wir im Norden. Die Halbinsel Cape York bietet eine herrliche Wildnis, ist aber etwas zu trocken und zu abgelegen. Die Möglichkeiten für Schule und Arbeit waren sehr begrenzt, Krankenhäuser weit entfernt und der Transport von Gütern eine echte Herausforderung.

Douglas Shire gefiel uns am besten. Die Fahrt nördlich von Cairns führt an den schönsten Küstengebieten des Landes vorbei. Saubere, menschenleere Strände und baumbewachsene Berge erstrecken sich entlang der Küste. Die perfekte Postkartenidylle der Küstenstraße gibt den Blick frei auf Zuckerrohrfelder und von Regenwald bedeckte Berge. Das Grün der Wildnis verliert sich in den Blautönen der Ferne. Das Zuckerrohranbaugebiet endet hier und macht großen Rinderfarmen Platz. Weiter nördlich, hinter dem Daintree River, werden die Farmen kleiner und dichter Regenwald wächst bis hinunter ans Meer. Bis jetzt hat sich die Natur hier größtenteils behauptet.

Johnston River Lookout

For us this was the end of 'civilisation' and the edge of the beyond. It was the point where we could still function in society, yet be 'mothered' by the earth. Sometimes in life you just know where you are meant to be, and we knew this area was for us.

We proceeded to look for land throughout the Douglas Shire. Every weekend we would travel and visit as many sites as was possible, searching for that magic spot. We found our land as early as 1978, but alas the timing wasn't right. We continued to search and saw amazing places - along crocodile inhabited creeks to almost vertical forested hillsides. We even placed an ad in the local paper offering a reward for anyone who could find us that perfect 'paradise'.

Hier befanden wir uns am Rande der Zivilisation, der Schnittstelle, wo wir noch in der Gesellschaft integriert waren, aber trotzdem im Herzen der Natur leben konnten. Manchmal im Leben spürt man genau wo man hingehört. Hier wussten wir sofort: dieser Ort war wie für uns geschaffen.

Also suchten wir von nun an in der Region von Douglas Shire nach "unserem" Land. Jedes Wochenende besichtigten wir so viele Plätze wie nur möglich, immer auf der Suche nach dem »Magic Spot«. Wir fanden unser Land bereits 1978, aber die Zeit war wohl noch nicht reif. So suchten wir weiter und fanden die verrücktesten Plätze, teils mit Bächen, in denen Krokodile lebten, oder senkrecht abfallenden Gebirgswäldern. Wir setzten eine Suchanzeige in die örtliche Zeitung und boten eine Belohnung für denjenigen, der uns das perfekte "Paradies" zeigen konnte.

The Devils Thumb

Early morning at the Botanical Ark

The beginnings

When we first acquired our land in 1982 it was virtually treeless. We had purchased it from cattle farmers who burned the land each year to keep the shrubs from coming back. What we inherited was lots of grass, weeds and erosion gullies and an immense amount of work..

The land was originally surveyed in 1928, and shortly thereafter it was turned into a sugar cane farm. In those early days, sugar cane was grown, by hand, on the hills, and on the dissected and terraced creek banks and foothills. Mechanical harvesting developed, with the Mossman Mill as one of the pioneers of this new technology, and sugar moved from the hills to the flat land, which in our valley was scarce. Neighbouring farmers had the same problems of ensuring viability, and decided to purchase a bulldozer and create as much flat land as possible. Hills and ridges were bulldozed and gullies and low lying areas filled in. The harvesting machines got bigger and eventually the farms became too small for sugar. The land was sold to cattle farmers from Daintree, from whom we purchased it.

Our first priority was to implement soil conservation measures to stop the erosion - the loss of an integral part of any future on the land. Days of digging and picking up rocks turned into weeks, weeks into months and many years later we are still picking up (and utilising) the rocks. We began implementing better conservation methods and saving more of our precious resources. We raised and employed millions of earthworms to try and replenish the topsoil, and commenced planting trees - the ultimate saviour of soils on (any) sloping lands.

Als wir unser Land 1982 übernahmen, war es praktisch baumlos. Wir hatten es von einem Rinderzüchter gekauft, der das Land jedes Jahr abbrannte, um es von Sträuchern frei zu halten. So bekamen wir sehr viel Gras, Unkraut, Erosionskanäle und jede Menge Arbeit ...

Das Land war urspünglich 1928 begutachtet und gleich darauf in eine Zuckerrohrfarm verwandelt worden. In jenen frühen Jahren wurde das Zuckerrohr von Hand angebaut. Meist auf Hügeln, terrassierten Flussufern und unterhalb von Bergen. Erntemaschinen wurden entwickelt, die Mossman Zuckerfabrik war eine der Pioniere dieser neuen Technik. Der Zuckerrohranbau verlagerte sich von den Hügeln in die Ebene. Flaches Land war aber knapp in unserem Tal. Die Nachbarfarmen hatten die gleichen Probleme mit der Wirtschaftlichkeit und kauften eine Planierraupe, um möglichst viel ebenes Terrain zu schaffen. Hügel und Raine wurden eingeebnet, Bachläufe und Senken aufgefüllt. Die Erntemaschinen wurden größer und schließlich waren die Farmen zu klein für den Zuckerrohranbau. Das Land wurde an Viehzüchter von Daintree verkauft, von denen wir es erwarben.

Von Anfang an war unser Hauptanliegen, den Boden vor Erosion zu schützen. Denn Erosion bedeutet den Verlust jeglicher Grundlage für das Lebens in und mit der Natur. Tage mit Graben und Steine sammeln wurden zu Wochen. Und Wochen zu Monaten. Und viele Jahre später lesen wir immer noch Steine auf - und nutzen sie sinnvoll. Wir führten bessere Bodenschutzmethoden ein und bewahrten zunehmend unsere kostbaren Ressourcen. Wir züchteten Millionen von Regenwürmern und setzten sie aus, um die Erdkrume an der Oberfläche zu verbessern. Auch pflanzten wir weiter Bäume. Sie sind der bestmögliche Erosionschutz bei abfallendem Gelände.

Botanical Ark 1980 ...

... the aerialview in 2000

The beginnings # 2

Our move into the valley saw us at first stay in a nearby stone barracks, a remnant from the days when cane cutters toiled on the hills cutting the crop by hand. It was a home of sorts, where one could see the stars through the holes in the roof on a clear night, or have the compulsory shower on a rainy one. There was no electricity, or hot water or running water (except when it rained). Not even a toilet.

So the challenges of our young family (our children Heather & Cali, were 4 and 2, respectively) started with repairing our »new« old home on the adjacent land.

The Carle family 1984

The first few years were hard, but exciting. We had to work for others to pay off the land and the needs that families have. We improved the barracks with the essential services, constructed a plant nursery and began planting our orchards. In our spare time we commenced preparations for our future home.

The very early beginnings

Nach unserer Ankunft im Tal zogen wir zunächst in eine Steinbaracke, zurückgelassen von den Zuckerrohrarbeitern der frühen Jahre. Es war eine jener Unterkünfte, von denen aus man in klaren Nächten durch die Löcher im Dach die Sterne sehen konnte - oder bei Regen eine unfreiwillige Dusche abbekam. Es gab keinen Strom, kein heißes oder gar fließendes Wasser (außer bei Regen), ja nicht einmal eine Toilette.

So begannen die Herausforderungen an unsere junge Familie (Heather und Cali waren 4 und 2 Jahre) mit der Reparatur unseres neuen "alten" Heims.

Die ersten Jahre waren anstrengend aber auch aufregend. Wir mussten für andere arbeiten, um unser Land abzubezahlen und die Familie zu versorgen. Wir statteten die Baracke mit dem Nötigsten aus, bauten eine Gärtnerei und begannen, unseren Obstgarten anzupflanzen. In der knappen Freizeit fuhren wir mit der Planung unseres zukünftigen Zuhauses fort.

The Carle family home

The Carle family home

The beginnings #3

We designed our house ourselves. We wanted breakfast in the sun, and a house that was part of the garden, not separate from it. We wanted it to funnel the breezes that seemed to ebb away on the sultry summer days and to catch the cool mountain air in the bedrooms at night.

It needed to be a functional house, and one that we could afford. We wanted openings everywhere- to lighten and brighten and to savour the fresh air.

In addition to our other jobs we slowly commenced building. Trying to do everything, we soon realised, would take a lifetime for the two of us. We then engaged a couple of block-layers to lay the walls and in no time we had the shell of the house. From then on, it gradually transformed into a home. Nineteen years after commencing we are still slowly working on it. But it feels great and fulfils those dreams we had dreamt.

We can remember the day when we moved into our home. In the past the children never really had any of the 'conveniences'. Now they were forever turning light switches on and off and flushing the toilets - how we take so much for granted.

Wir entwarfen unser Haus selbst. Wir wollten in der Morgensonne frühstücken und ein Haus, das Teil des Gartens ist und nicht davon getrennt . Wir wollten, dass es die Brise einfing, die besonders an schwülen Sommertagen ganz zu verebben drohte und die des nachts die kühle Bergluft in den Schlafzimmer hielt.

Es musste ein praktisches Haus sein und natürlich eines, das wir uns leisten konnten. Wir wollten überall Öffnungen - für Licht, Großzügigkeit, und um die frische Luft in vollen Zügen in uns aufzusaugen.

Wegen unserer vielen anderen Aufgaben kamen wir mit dem Hausbau nur langsam voran. Wir merkten schon bald, dass es für uns zwei eine Lebensaufgabe sein würde, wollten wir es ganz alleine schaffen. So beauftragten wir ein paar Maurer und in kürzester Zeit stand der Rohbau. Diesen verwandelten wir von nun an schrittweise in ein Zuhause. Neunzehn Jahre später sind wir noch immer nicht ganz fertig. Aber das Erreichte gibt uns ein großartiges Gefühl und ist die Erfüllung unserer Träume.

Wir können uns noch gut an den Umzug in unser neues Heim erinnern. Bis dahin verfügten die Kinder noch über keine der sonst üblichen Annehmlichkeiten. Nun schalteten sie ständig die Lichter an und aus und betätigten die Toilettenspülung. - wie leicht nehmen wir doch so vieles für selbstverständlich hin.

Alan studied marine biology

Cali, Suzi, Alan and Heather Carle

Tropical Fruits General

Tropical rainforests have managed to conserve and conceal hundreds, if not thousands, of different fruits and nuts from most of the world's inhabitants.

The Botanical Ark is one of only a few institutions or individuals trying to raise awareness and challenge (enlighten) the tastebuds for the rest of us.

Our quest to feed our family started with the plan to get our long term crops in the ground first- that is the fruits and nuts- our tree crops. When we saw what was available in the way of fruits suitable for our climate we realised there had to be more. Local nurseries at the time tried to even sell us apples and pears, peaches and grapes!

One basic 'rule' of living on the land is to grow crops suitable to our environment. If we don't, we will pay a heavy price for trying and ultimately fail. The equation became simple - if you live in a tropical rainforest environment - grow tropical rainforest trees.

We had the idea that some interesting fruits grew in the South East Asian rainforests. How could we get them here?

Our first attempt to source these new fruits was by correspondence and contact with like-minded individuals. We managed to find a few people interested in 'exotic' fruits and learned of an organization overseas called the Rare Fruit Council. We had our first leads and embarked on a journey that would take us (so far) to more than 40 countries on 5 continents and isolated islands.

Den tropischen Regenwäldern ist es gelungen, hunderte, wenn nicht tausende verschiedener Früchte und Nüsse zu erhalten und vor den meisten Erdbewohnern zu verbergen.

Die Botanical Ark gehört zu den wenigen Institutionen bzw. Privatpersonen, die versuchen, das Bewusstsein auf diese verborgenen Schätze zu lenken und unser aller Geschmacksknospen wachzukitzeln.

Seedling

In unserem Bemühen, die Familie zu ernähren, pflanzten wir zuerst die langsam wachsenden Frucht- und Nussbäume an. Als wir sahen, welche Fruchtplanzen für unser Klima angeboten wurden, dachten wir, dass es da doch noch mehr geben müsse. Die örtlichen Gärtnereien wollten uns damals sogar Äpfel, Birnen, Pfirsiche und Weintrauben verkaufen!

Eine wichtige Erkenntnis für das Leben in der Natur war für uns: Baue nur Pflanzen an, die zur Klimazone passen. Wer sich nicht dran hält, zahlt einen hohen Preis fürs Ausprobieren und wird dennoch scheitern. Die Gleichung ist daher einfach - wer im tropischen Regenwald lebt, pflanze tropische Bäume an!

Wir wussten von einigen interessanten Obstsorten, die in den Regenwäldern Süd-Ost-Asiens wuchsen - aber wie sollten wir diese hierher bekommen?

Der erste Ansatz, neue Pflanzen zu bekommen, lief über den Kontakt zu Gleichgesinnten. Wir fanden einige Leute, die Interesse an exotischen Früchten hatten, und erfuhren von einer Organisation in Übersee, die sich "Rare Fruit Council" nannte. Dies gab uns weitere Anhaltspunkte und wir machten uns auf eine (Lebens)Reise, die uns bis heute in mehr als 40 Länder auf 5 Kontinenten und auf viele einsame Inseln geführt hat.

Cola species / Central Africa

The first couple of years saw us expand our meagre collection by about 25 new species! We were overjoyed.

Our inquisitive nature asked "if there are 25 new fruits from a small part of South East Asia, what might we find in the world's largest rainforest - The Amazon?

The leads were few and research materials scarce - so we decided that perhaps we should go and take a look ourselves- discover if and what might be worth bringing back to Australia.

Our first trip took us to the South-West Pacific, on to Hawaii and down through Central America to South America. We flew up to Florida where our first daughter Heather was born and then back down to the Amazon. For 11 months that year we discovered, tasted and collected fruits we never knew existed. By the time we arrived home, we had shipped back or brought with us more than 80 new species of fruits and nuts!

Within just a few years we had been able to acquire more than 100 new types of fruits. But our curiosity kept delving and we wondered what the people we had visited ate for the rest of the year- after all, we had only been with them for a few days.

One trip led to another and by 2001 we had made many trips - back and forth to the jungles of South and Central America, through parts of the West Indies, into South East Asia, from Burma to Borneo, Thailand, Indonesia, Malaysia, into Papua New Guinea, southern India and even more remote areas like West and Central Africa and Madagascar.

We have faced adversity, illness, muggings and mayhem, and yet the friends we made along the way will always be in our hearts and minds. As our trees begin to produce these new fruits we remember the good times and share those memories (and fruits) with others.

In den ersten beiden Jahren vergrößerte sich unsere spärliche Sammlung um 25 neue Arten! Wir waren überglücklich.

Wissbegierig, wie wir waren, fragten wir uns: Wenn wir in einer kleinen Region Süd-Ost-Asiens bereits 25 neue Obstsorten entdeckten, was würden wir dann wohl im größten Regenwald der Erde vorfinden - im Amazonas?

Es gab wenig konkrete Hinweise und auch Forschungsergebnisse waren rar. So beschlossen wir, uns selbst auf den Weg zu machen und herauszufinden, ob es etwas gab, das es wert war, nach Australien eingeführt zu werden.

Die erste Reise führte uns zum Süd-West-Pazifik, weiter nach Hawaii, durch Mittelamerika und nach Südamerika. Wir flogen nach Florida, wo unsere Tochter Heather geboren wurde, und dann wieder zurück an den Amazonas. In 11 Monaten dieses Jahres entdeckten, kosteten und sammelten wir Früchte, von deren Existenz wir nie gehört hatten. Bis wir zuhause ankamen, hatten wir mehr als 80 neue Arten von Früchten und Nüssen vorausgeschickt oder mitgebracht!

Innerhalb weniger Jahre hatten wir demnach mehr als 100 neue Sorten hinzugewonnen. Aber unser Wissensdurst war noch immer nicht gestillt. Wir fragten uns, was die Leute, die wir besucht hatten, in all den anderen Jahreszeiten aßen - wir hatten sie ja jeweils nur wenige Tage besucht.

Eine Reise reihte sich an die nächste und bis 2001 waren es schon eine ganze Menge. Wir reisten kreuz und quer durch die Urwälder Süd- und Mittelamerikas, durch Teile Westindiens, nach Süd-Ost-Asien, von Burma nach Borneo, Thailand, Indonesien, Malaysia bis nach Papua Neuguinea, Südindien und auch zu noch abgelegeneren Gebieten wie West- und Zentralafrika und Madagaskar.

Wir erlebten widrige Zeiten, Krankheiten, selbst Überfälle mit schwerer Körperverletzung und doch überwiegen die positiven Erinnerungen an die Freundschaften, die wir entlang unseres Weges schlossen bei weitem. Seit wir nun die eigenen exotischen Früchte von den damals entdeckten Bäumen geniessen, teilen wir alte Erinnerungen und natürlich die leckeren Früchte mit unseren zahlreichen Besuchern.

Local bearing gift

Norbert and Bettina Guthier, Bedas, Suzi and Alan Carle

Fruits from America ...

South and Central American rainforests have provided the world with fruits we will always expect to find in the shops. They include the pineapple, avocado, brazil nuts and the papaya.

Our culture would indeed be poorer without the cacao (Theobroma cacao). Chocolate drinks and sweets, all of which originate from cacao, enrich our diet and lifestyles.

Lesser known fruits take an ever increasing space on the market shelves as we become aware of their unique characteristics and tastes.

- The yellow pitaya (Cereus triangularis) fruit comes from a climbing cactus that produces spectacular night blooms. The yellow fruits have a firm yet juicy edible centre which is translucent with hundreds of tiny jet black edible seeds. A fresh chilled pitaya is one of the very finest dessert fruits.

- Mammea (Mammea americana) comes from a tall luxuriant evergreen tree and produces grapefruit-sized fruits whose firm flesh resembles apricot marmalade.

- Caimitos or star apples (Chrysophyllum cainito) are produced on large spreading trees with a brilliant bronze underneath to the foliage. The 7-10cm (3-4") fruits are either purple, green or bronze and the internal flesh combines two textures in a delicate blend of milky sweetness.

Die süd- und zentralamerikanischen Regenwälder haben der Welt Früchte geschenkt, von denen wir heutzutage erwarten, sie in Obstgeschäften vorzufinden. Unter anderem sind dies Ananas, Avocados, Brazilnüsse und Papayas.

Unsere Kultur wäre ohne den Kakaobaum (Theobroma cacao) um einiges ärmer. Schokogetränke und Süßigkeiten, die mit Kakao hergestellt sind, bereichern unsere Ernährung und unseren Lebensstil.

Weniger bekannte Früchte bekommen immer mehr Marktanteile, seit wir ihre Besonderheiten und Geschmacksvarianten kennen.

- Die gelbe Pitaya (Cereus triangularis) kommt von einem rankenden Kaktus, der spektakuläre Blüten in der Nacht ausbildet. Die gelbe Frucht hat ein festes, saftiges, durchscheinendes Inneres, das mit hunderten kleinen, ebenfalls essbaren schwarzen Kernen gefüllt ist. Eine frisch geschälte Pitaya ist eine der besten Früchte als Dessert.

- Mammea (Mammea americana) kommt von einem grossen, üppig wachsenden, immergrünen Baum, dessen grapefruchtgrossen Früchte mit ihrem festen Fruchtfleisch an Aprikosenmarmelade erinnern.

- Caimitos oder Sternfrucht (Chrysophyllum cainito) wachsen auf weit ausladenden Bäumen, deren Blattunterseiten bronzefarben glänzen. Die 7-10 cm grossen Früchte sind entweder violett, grün oder bronzefarben und das innere Fruchtfleich kombiniert zwei Texturen, eine delikate Mischung aus milchiger Süsse.

Yellow Pitaya

Mammea

Cacao

Caimito

White cockatoo feeds on a papaya.

Mamey sapote (Pouteria sapota) has its origins in Central America. The rough-skin of this large 10-20cm (4-8") fruit protects one of the sweetest, richest fruits imaginable. The smooth orange pulp is able to provide sustenance, or enrich and flavour ice creams, drinks and pastries. (see recipes)

- Rollinia (Rollinia deliciosa) is common in the Amazon where the 10-25cm (4-10") bumpy yellow fruits are relished. The melt-in-your-mouth white flesh is a delicate blend of sweetness with a hint of lemon sub-acidity.

- Zapote' is an Aztec word for fruit, so many Central American fruits have retained this connection.The black sapote, sometimes called chocolate pudding fruit (Diospyros digyna) is a relative of the persimmon. The smooth and soft black/brown pulp can be eaten fresh or made into delightful puddings, drinks and sweets.

- Ingas or guamas (sometimes called ice-cream beans) (Inga species) come in many different shapes and sizes and the mainly green or brownish fruits contain a sweet and moist, yet somewhat fibrous pulp surrounding each of the seeds within the pod. Related to beans, these trees often exhibit exceptional growth rates - occasionally up to 5m (16') each year!

- Pejibaye (Bactris gasipaes) generally grow on spiny palms and have been labelled the 'tree of life' by some of the people that rely on this important food to feed their families.

There are many kinds of pejibaye, all of which provide very nutritious fruits that are cooked and made into dozens of important foods such as tortas and soups. The growing point of this palm also provides excellent 'palmito' or 'the heart of palm'. This delicacy was once called 'millionaire's salad' due to the fact the plant was usually killed to harvest this tender food. With pejibaye, the palm sends up suckers or shoots and can be harvested sustainably over many years. Other varieties of pejibaye are utilised for the oils in the fruits, and the leaves and stems are often used in building applications.

Mamey sapote (Pouteria sapota) kommt aus Zentralamerika. Die rauhe Schale der 10-20 cm großen Früchte umschliesst ein Fruchtfleisch, dass zu dem süssesten und gehaltvollsten gehört, was man sich vorstellen kann. Das weiche, orangene Fruchtfleisch hat einen hohen Nährwert und kann Speiseeis, Getränke und Gebäck aufwerten. (siehe Rezepte)

- Rollinia (Rollinia deliciosa) kommt aus dem Amazonasgebiet, wo sich die 10-25 cm grosse, knollige, gelbe Frucht äusserster Beliebheit erfreut. Das besonders zarte, weiße Fruchtfleisch schmeckt wie eine feine Mischung von Süssem und einem Hauch zitroniger Säure.

- Zapote ist das aztekische Wort für Frucht. Im Namen vieler mittelamerikanischer Früchte ist diese Abstammung noch heute zu entdecken. Die schwarze Zapote, manchmal auch Schokoladenpuddingfrucht genannt (Diospyros digyna) ist mit der Persimmon verwandt. Das glatte, weiche, schwarzbraune Fruchtfleisch kann roh gegessen oder zu Pudding, Getränken und Süssigkeiten verarbeitet werden.

- Ingas oder Guamas gibt es in vielen verschiedenen Formen und Grössen. Die meist grünen oder bräunlichen Früchte enthalten ein süsses und saftiges, jedoch eher faseriges Fruchtfleisch, das jeden einzelnen der Kerne innerhalb des Gehäuses umhüllt. Verwandt mit Bohnen, wachsen diese Bäume, mit bis zu fünf Metern pro Jahr, ausserordentlich schnell.

- Pejibaye (Bactris gasipaes) wachsen normalerweise als stachelige Palmen. Sie werden von einigen Leuten auch "Lebensbaum" genannt, da die Früchte für die Ernährung ihrer Familien eine große Bedeutung haben.

Es gibt viele Arten von Pejibaye, die sehr nahrhafte Früchte hervorbringen. Man kann diese kochen und zu dutzenden wichtigen Nahrungsmitteln, wie Fladenbrot und Suppen, weiterverarbeiten. Das Stamminnere dieser Palme nannte man früher auch "Millionärs-Salat", da die Palme bei der Ernte des zarten Gemüses gefällt wurde. Die Pejibaye - Palme treibt unterirdische Sprossen, die über viele Jahre hinweg geerntet werden können. Andere Pejibaye-Arten finden wegen des Öls in ihren Früchten Verwendung. Die Blätter und Stämme werden oft als Baumaterial genutzt.

Mamey Sapote

Rollinia

Black Sapote

Inga

Pejibaye palm

... South East Asia ...

South East Asia is the origin of hundreds of exciting fruits. Long recognised for their outstanding flavour and nutritional values by their local people, many of these have been carefully selected and nurtured for thousands of years.

We are all aware of some of the more common tropical fruits from this region, the banana, the mango, and some of the citrus.

- Petai (Parkia speciosa) is a bean from large forest trees and is an important flavouring ingredient in many asian meals.
- Duku (Lansium domesticum) is, in our opinion, one of the finest fruits of the 'old world tropics'. These 4-6cm (1.5-2.5") tan fruits encase a firm translucent flesh of delicate sweet-sub acid flavour.
- Bignay (Antidesma bunius) are small 8-10mm (3/8") red to purple acid fruits which make delightful jams, juices, and wine. The leaves are used in cooking and salads.
- Bananas (Musa hybrids) more than 400 different banana varieties and flavours exist. Used as dessert fruits or in cooking, the tropics wouldn't be the same without its most important fruit.
- Salak (Salacca zalacca) are one of the greatest surprises in Asian fruits. The 5-8cm (2-3") fruits appear to be covered in a thin but brittle snake skin. Remove the skin and the yellow/white firm flesh reminds us of a pineapple-flavoured granny smith apple.

Süd-Ost-Asien ist die Heimat von hunderten aufregenden Früchten. Seit langem werden sie von Einheimischen wegen ihres besonderen Geschmacks und ihres Nährwertes geschätzt, viele von ihnen sorgsam ausgewählt und seit tausenden von Jahren gezüchtet.

Wir sind alle vertraut mit den bekannten tropischen Früchten aus dieser Region, der Banane, der Mango und einigen Citrusarten.

- Petai (Parkia speciosa) ist die Bohne eines grossen Baumes und wichtiger Geschmacksträger von vielen asiatischen Gerichten.
- Duku (Lansium domesticum) ist unserer Meinung nach eine der besten tropischen Früchte. Diese 4-6 cm grosse, hellbraune Frucht beinhaltet ein festes, durchsichtiges Fruchtfleisch von delikatem süss - säuerlichem Geschmack.
- Bignay (Antidesma bunius) sind 8-10 mm kleine, säuerliche Früchte mit rot - violetter Schale, aus denen man köstliche Marmeladen, Säfte und Wein herstellen kann. Die Blätter werden beim Kochen und in Salaten verwendet.
- Bananen (Musa hybrids) gibt es in mehr als 400 verschiedene Arten und Geschacksrichtungen. Sie werden als Nachtisch oder zum Kochen verwendet. Die Tropen wären ohne diese wichtigste Frucht gar nicht vorstellbar.
- Salak (Salacca zalacca) ist eine der grössten Überraschungen unter den asiatischen Früchten. Die 5-8 cm grossen Früchte sind wie in eine dünne, zerbrechliche Schlangenhaut gehüllt. Geschält erinnert uns der Geschack des festen, gelblich-weissen Fruchtfleisches an einen Granny Smith Apfel mit Ananasgeschmack.

Petai

Duku

Bignay

Banana varieties

Salak palm

An interesting aspect of South East Asian markets, villages and forests is that the more one looks for different and unusual foods the more one finds.

Anyone who resides in South East Asia, even for a short time, would probably have seen such unusual fruits as the jackfruit (Artocarpus heterophyllus) (which has been known to reach 70 kg (150 lb) in size). This immense fruit yields a sweet, soft to firm, yellow aril surrounding each of the 50-100 seeds. This is eaten fresh or used as a flavouring. The mature seeds are boiled or roasted and provide a useful nut (see recipes- use as per champadek). The immature green fruits are often chopped and cooked as vegetable.

- The Menteng, Rambai and Tampoi (Baccaurea species) are found wild or cultivated for their sweet/sour juicy fruits. Rambai fruit hang from the trees like strings of pearls. Tampoi and Menteng cluster on the main trunks and branches.They are delightfully refreshing.

- Rambutans (Nephelium lappaceum) are one of the most commonly found fruits and beneath the soft red spines is a crisp sweet translucent flesh.

However, any mention of the fruits of this region must include the 'king' and 'queen' of fruits; the 'durian' and 'mangosteen'.

- Durian (Durio zibethinus) is the most notorious of fruits. The rich odour prevents many from eating this captivating fruit, yet those that venture past its exceedlingly sharp spines and smell can enjoy one of the richest finest fruits known to human and orangutan alike.

- Mangosteen (Garcinia mangostana) has often been called 'the finest fruit in existence'.The 7.5cm (3") dark purple fruits contain white segments of flesh that dissolve into your mouth with the most pleasant, delicate and sweet taste imaginable.

Some of the smells (aromas) and tastes can, at first, seem overbearing or unusual. With time, the tropics manages to blend and mix those sensory extremes into a fascinating culture. So integral to Asia are these fruits that the smell of just one piece can trigger a longing for the far east and it's enticing cuisine.

Ein interessanter Aspekt der süd-ost-asiatischen Märkte, Dörfer und Wälder ist, je mehr man nach anderen, ungewöhnlichen Lebensmitteln sucht, desto mehr entdeckt man auch.

Jeder, der auch nur für kurze Zeit in Süd-Ost-Asien gelebt hat, wird solch ungewöhnliche Früchte wie die Jackfruit (Artocarpus heterophyllus), die bis zu 70 kg schwer werden kann, gesehen haben. Diese riesige Frucht liefert eine süsse, gelbliche, weiche bis feste Masse, die die etwa 50-100 Samenkörner umschließt. Man kann sie roh essen oder zur Geschmacksverbesserung nutzen. Nachdem sie gekocht oder geröstet wurden, sind die reifen Kerne ähnlich wie Nüsse (siehe Rezept Champadek). Die unreifen, grünen Früchte werden oft klein geschnitten und als Gemüse zubereitet.

- Die Menteng, Rambai und Tampoi (Baccaurea species) findet man wildwachsend, sie werden aber wegen ihrer süss-sauren, saftigen Frucht auch angebaut. Die Rambaifrüchte hängen wie Perlenschüre von den Bäumen. Tampoi und Menteng wachsen in Trauben an den Stämmen und Ästen. Sie sind köstlich und erfrischend.

- Rambutans (Nephelium lappaceum) gehören zu den bekanntesten Früchten. Unter den weichen, roten Dornen verbirgt sich ihr knackiges, süßes und halbtransparentes Fruchtfleisch.

Natürlich dürfen bei keiner Aufzählung der Früchte dieser Region der "König" und die "Königin" der Früchte fehlen: "Duiran" und "Mangosteen".

- Durian (Durio zibethinus) ist die berühmtberüchtigste Frucht von allen. Ihr starker Geruch hält viele davon ab, diese interessante Frucht zu probieren. Alle, die sich von ihren außerordentlich scharfen Dornen und dem starken Geruch nicht abhalten lassen, erfreuen sich an einer der köstlichsten Früchte, die den Menschen - und den Orang-Utans - bekannt sind.

- Mangosteen (Garcinia mangostana) wird oft auch als die "edelste existierende Frucht" bezeichet. Die 7,5 cm großen, dunkel-violetten Früchte enthalten weiße Fruchtfleischsegmente. Im Mund schmelzen diese dahin und setzen ein feines, unvorstellbar köstlichsüsses Aroma frei.

Einige der Gerüche, Aromen und Geschmacksrichtungen mögen einem zunächst etwas aufdringlich oder ungewohnt erscheinen. Aber mit der Zeit gelingt es den Tropen, diesen extremen Reiz der Sinne zu einer faszinierenden Kultur zu verschmelzen. Diese Früchte repräsentieren Asien so sehr, dass schon der Duft eines kleinen Stückchens ausreichen kann, um die Sehnsucht nach dem fernen Osten und seiner verführerischen Küche auszulösen.

Jackfruit

Menteng, Rambai, Tamoi

Durian

Rambutan

Mangosteen

... Africa, Madagascar ...

The jungles of Africa often conjure up visions of gorillas, pygmies and sometimes Tarzan and Jane. Dense jungles covered much of the equatorial regions and still remain in remote places. Can you imagine your world without coffee or cola? Africa has provided us with the origins, not only for the human race, but some of the most important (and addictive) beverages as well. Coffee satisfies the caffine cravings of many hundreds of millions of people each day. And Cola tree seeds are one major part of a famous drink that quenches our thirst and stimulates our nervous system.

A walk through the rainforests of Africa and Madagascar will introduce even the keenest of fruit growers to a whole new world of tropical fruits and nuts. The names Itanga, Safu, Ngutukpana, Kaso, Eta and Bolongo don't mean much to most people outside the Congo, yet these are important forest fruits in one of the world's largest remaining rainforests. Trek deep into these jungles and you may uncover numerous wild relatives of these locally common fruits - many of which are just as exciting and interesting.

- Itanga or Safu (Dacryodes edulis) is one of the most important fruits of Central Africa's rain forests. The 4-12cm (2-5") mainly purple fruits are soaked in hot water to soften and used as a vegetable, taste a bit like a sour avocado.

- Ngutukpana (Salacia species) is a very interesting orange/red bumpy fruit 7.5 cm (3") long with a translucent orange pulp that is wonderfully sweet.

- Kaso (Tetracarpidium conophorum) grow on a vine and the 7.5cm (3") fruits produce 4-5 large and hard seeds which need to be boiled or roasted before eating. They are generally eaten with meals.

- Eta (Landolphia species) many varieties occur within the forests. This one 10cm (4") in diameter, has a sweet/sub acid flesh surrounding the 20 or so seeds.

- Bolongo (Maesobotrya staudii) protrude like bunches of small 8mm (1/3")red/orange grapes from the trunks of rainforest trees. The outside skin splits open to reveal a sweet/sour scant pulp around each seed. Interesting and refreshing.

Unter Afrika´s Urwald stellen wir uns oft Gorillas, Pygmäen und vielleicht auch mal Tarzan und Jane vor. Undurchdringlicher Dschungel bedeckte zum größten Teil die Regionen entlang des Äquators. Wir finden ihn noch immer in entlegenen Gegenden. Können Sie sich ein Leben ohne Kaffee und Cola vorstellen? Afrika ist nicht nur die Wiege der Menschheit, sondern auch der bedeutendsten abhängig machenden Getränke überhaupt. Kaffee befriedigt täglich das Koffeinverlangen von mehreren hundert Millionen Menschen. Die Samen des Colabaumes sind der Hauptbestandteil eines berühmten Erfrischungsgetränkes, das unseren Durst löscht und unser Nervensystem stimuliert.

Ein Gang durch die Regenwälder Afrikas und Madagaskars wird auch dem leidenschaftlichsten Obstbauer eine völlig neue Welt tropischer Früchte und Nüsse offenbaren. Die Namen Itanga, Safu, Ngutukpana, Kaso, Eta und Bolongo bedeuten für Leute außerhalb des Kongo wenig, jedoch handelt es sich dabei um wichtige Waldfrüchte aus einem der größten verbliebenen Regenwälder der Erde. Wenn Sie tief in den Dschungel vordringen würden, könnten Sie leicht unzählige wilde Verwandte dieser dort regional bekannten Früchte entdecken, viele genauso aufregend wie interessant.

- Itanga oder Safu (Dacryodes edulis) ist eine der wichtigsten Früchte des zentralafrikanischen Regenwaldes. Die 4-12 cm großen, meist violetten Früchte werden in heissem Wasser aufgeweicht und als Gemüse gegessen, das ein wenig wie säuerliche Avocados schmeckt.

- Ngutukpana (Salacia species) ist eine sehr interessante, orange-rote, bauchige Frucht. Sie ist etwa 7,5 cm lang und ihr halbtransparentes, orangefarbiges Fruchtfleisch schmeckt wunderbar süss.

- Kaso (Tetracarpidium conophorum) wächst an einer Kletterpflanze. Die 7,5 cm lange Frucht bringt 4-5 grosse Samenkörner hervor, die vor dem Essen gekocht oder geröstet werden müssen. Sie werden gewöhnlich zu Mahlzeiten gereicht.

- Eta (Landolphia species) kommt im Regenwald in vielen Arten vor. Die im Durchmesser 10 cm messende Frucht hat ca. 20 Kerne, die von süss-säuerlichem Fruchtfleisch umgeben sind.

- Bolongo (Maesobotrya staudii) treten wie 8 mm kleine Büschel rot-oranger Trauben aus den Stämmen der Regenwaldbäume hervor. Wenn die Aussenhaut aufplatzt, enthüllt sie ein wenig süss-saures Fruchtfleisch, das jeden Kern umschliesst. Interessant und erfrischend.

Itanga or Safu

Ngutukpana, Salacia sp.

Kaso, tetracarpidium sp.

Eta

'Bolongo' Maesobotrya staudii

... Pacific and Australia.

One cannot visit the South Pacific and fail to be enchanted by the coconut palms and the breadfruit trees. Both are integral to the landscape and the diet of almost every pacific islander.

Walk into the forests of the major islands and you will find fruits that have sustained and nourished the local populations for thousands of years. Exciting and unusual fruits that, for the most part, seem to have remained secreted by the vast ocean that surrounds these special places.

One could be excused for thinking macadamia nuts originated in Hawaii. Unless, of course, you come from Australia, the real home of the famous mac nuts.

Aborigines traversed the rainforests of this distant land for tens of thousands of years, harvesting fruits and nuts on their journeys.

- Bunya Nuts (Araucaria bidwillii) come from Australia and the cones can weigh 8 kg (18lb.) The large 4cm (1.5") nuts are roasted and eaten by aborigines and sold in the growing native foods market.

- Dawa or Taun (Pometia pinnata) occurs throughout the Western Pacific and produces bunches of 2-4cm (1-1.5") fruits, either green, yellow, purple, red or black. The thin brittle skin encases a sweet juicy translucent flesh that locals relish.

- Buk-buk (Burckella obovata) occurs in Papua New Guinea and the 100-150mm 4-6") green fruits contain a sweet milky pulp. Pandanus (Pandanus species) occur throughout the Pacific and different species are eaten in varying ways. In some the seeds are edible, in others only the flesh. Pandanus leaves are important in weaving matting and baskets.

- Breadfruit (Artocarpus altilis) is the most important fruit growing at The Botanical Ark. Traditionally it is cooked in earthen ovens when green, and eaten fresh when ripe. It can be made into soups, breads, chips, pasta (see recipes), pastries and puddings

Es ist unmöglich, den Südpazifik zu besuchen, ohne von den Kokospalmen und Breadfruit-Bäumen begeistert zu sein. Beide bestimmen ganz wesentlich das Landschaftsbild und den Speiseplan nahezu aller Inselbewohner.

Streifen Sie durch die Wälder der Hauptinseln, und Sie treffen auf die Früchte, welche die Einheimischen schon seit Jahrtausenden ernähren. Es sind überraschende und ungewöhnliche Früchte, die scheinbar bislang weitgehend unentdeckt geblieben sind. Dies mag an dem riesigen, diese Inseln umgebenden Ozean liegen. Es sei Ihnen verziehen, wenn Sie glauben, dass die Macadamia Nüsse aus Hawaii stammen. Außer natürlich, Sie kommen aus Australien, der eigentlichen Heimat dieser berühmten "Mac Nuts".

Aborigines durchquerten schon vor zehntausenden von Jahren diese fernen Regenwälder und ernteten dort Früchte und Nüsse.

- Bunya Nuts (Araucaria bidwillii) stammen aus Australien. Ihre Zapfen können bis zu 8 kg wiegen. Die 4 cm großen Nüsse werden von Aborigines gerne geröstet gegessen und heute auch auf dem wachsenden Markt für einheimische Produkte angeboten.

- Dawa or Taun (Pometia pinnata) kommt überall im Westpazifik vor. Die 2-4 cm grossen Früchte wachsen in Büscheln und sind grün, gelb, violett, rot oder schwarz. Die dünne, brüchige Haut umschliesst ein süsses, saftiges, halbtransparentes Fruchtfleisch, das den Einheimischen ganz besonders schmeckt.

- Buk-buk (Burckella obovata) kommt vor allem auf Neuguinea vor. Seine 10-15 cm großen, grünen Früchte haben ein süsses, milchiges Fruchtfleisch. Pandanus (Pandanus species) gibt es überall in der Pazifikregion. Die verschiedenen Arten werden in mannigfaltiger Weise genutzt. Bei einigen Arten sind die Samen essbar, bei anderen das Fruchtfleisch. Pandanusblätter finden beim Flechten von Matten und Körben Verwendung.

- Breadfruit (Artocarpus altilis) ist die wichtigste auf der Botanical Ark wachsende Frucht. Noch grün, wird sie traditionell im Lehmofen gegart, reif ganz einfach roh gegessen. Man kann sie zu Suppen, Brot, Chips und Nudeln verarbeiten oder zu Gebäck und Pudding.

Bunya Nuts

Dawa or Taun

Buk Buk

Pandanus

Breadfruit

The Botanical Ark Fruits

The Botanical Ark has an ever expanding collection of tropical fruits and nuts, and over the past 25 years of collections, we have sourced upwards of 400 different species. Sometimes we work alone, and sometimes in cooperation with other people who have common interests. Together we have created a truly remarkable collection.

Some of the finest tasting fruits have gone on to be cultivated by commercial growers, others await yet someone else's 'discoveries', and some remain solely in our botanical collections.

We try to visit rainforest areas of the world which are high in biodiversity, and which are highly threatened. We will often work with regional universities, botanic gardens and indigenous peoples to identify wild fruits and their potentially useful relatives.

The Botanical Ark is not the conservation 'failsafe' for any of these fruits and nuts. If we as a people truly value what nature has provided then we must attempt to preserve natural ecosystems. We must work with both governments and indigenous peoples to ensure values are recognised that will over-ride destructive developments.

The Botanical Ark is evolving into an educational facility which aims to increase an awareness for the long term conservation of these valuable species.

Die Botanical Ark verfügt über eine ständig wachsende Sammlung tropischer Früchte und Nüsse. In den vergangenen 25 Jahren haben wir mehr als 400 verschiedene Arten zusammengetragen. Machmal arbeiten wir alleine, zeitweise aber auch in Kooperation mit anderen, die unsere Interessen teilen.

Ein paar der geschmacklich besten Früchte werden inzwischen von kommerziellen Anbauern kultiviert, einige Arten warten noch auf ihre Entdecker und andere bleiben einzig und alleine in unserer eigenen botanischen Sammlung.

Wir besuchen und erkunden hauptsächlich bedrohte Regenwälder mit hoher Artenvielfalt auf der ganzen Welt. Dort arbeiten wir oft mit den örtlichen Universitäten, botanischen Gärten und der einheimischen Bevölkerung zusammen, um Wildfrüchte und deren eventuell nützliche Verwandte zu finden und zu bestimmen.

Die Botanical Ark ist kein Garant für den Erhalt der gesammelten Arten. Wenn wir als Menschen wirklich wertschätzen, welche Reichtümer uns die Natur mit den tropischen Früchten und Nüssen beschert, müssen wir versuchen, deren Herkunftswälder zu schützen. Wir müssen mit den Regierungen und der einheimischen Bevölkerung sprechen, um sicher zu stellen, dass vorhandene Werte erkannt und möglicherweise zerstörerische Entwicklungen aufgehalten werden.

Die Botanical Ark entwickelt sich zu einer Ausbildungsstätte, die darauf abzielt, das Bewusstsein verstärkt auf den Langzeitschutz dieser wertvollen Arten zu lenken.

Miracle Fruit

Mixed fruit at the Botanical Ark

Flowers

At the age of 19, I was crossing the Pacific, on my way to Australia. I stopped in Western Samoa, staying two weeks with a local Samoan family. On one occasion I had the opportunity to visit Aggie Grey's Hotel, and there I saw an incredible tropical flower. It was red and yellow and green, and waxy and large and had leaves like bananas do. The flower was hanging from this large plant right at eye level. The magic of this flower was to forever impact on this unsuspecting admirer. This was a heliconia!

In 1978, on a trip to South America to seek out new fruits, I again saw these unusual flowers and observed hummingbirds feeding on the nectar. A few of these colourful flowers had bold blue fruits extended skyward, inviting me (and I guess the birds) to take the seeds and distribute them. I did just that.

Growing fruit take time. We were told that some of our trees may take 20-30 years to fruit. The first mangosteen in Queensland actually took 22 years! Could we starve to death growing fruit? We soon realised we needed some other source of income until our trees began to produce.

Mit 19 Jahren überquerte ich den Pazifik auf meinem Weg nach Australien. Dabei hatte ich einen zweiwöchigen Aufenthalt bei einer einheimischen Familie auf Westsamoa. Es ergab sich ein Besuch des Aggie Grey´s Hotels. Dort sah ich eine unglaubliche tropische Blume. Sie war wachsig, rot, gelb und grün und hatte grosse Blätter, ähnlich denen einer Bananenstaude. Die Blüte hing von der riesigen Pflanze genau bis auf Augenhöhe herab. Sie verzauberte mich auf Anhieb und hinterliess einen sehr tiefen Eindruck. Die Pflanze war eine Helikonie!

Südamerika 1978, auf einer Exkursion, um neue Früchte zu entdecken, sah ich diese ungewöhnlichen Blumen erneut und beobachtete Kolibris beim Nektarsammeln. Einige dieser bunten Blüten hatten kräftige blaue Früchte, die sich himmelwärts reckten. Diese schienen mich (und wohl auch die Vögel) geradezu einzuladen, davon ein paar Samen mitzunehmen und zu verstreuen. Und genau das tat ich dann auch.

Fruchtpflanzen zu züchten, erfordert Zeit. Wir erfuhren, dass einige unserer Bäume 20-30 Jahre brauchen, bevor sie Früchte tragen würden. Und tatsächlich benötigten die ersten Magosteens in Queensland 22 Jahre! Sollten wir also verhungern, während wir Früchte anbauten? Wir sahen ein, dass wir eine andere Einnahmequelle brauchten, bis die Bäume zu tragen begannen.

Heliconia silvestris

Heliconia x Dinosaur

Travellers »palm«

Heliconia Psittacorum Lady Di

Heliconia rostrata

Three or four types of heliconia had already been grown in Australia before we began introducing new species and varieties. So well were they suited to growing in our area that they produced early and abundantly and many produced continuously. Admiration in the garden is nice, but it seemed logical to cut the flowers and bring them inside to admire for longer periods- and to brighten up the home.

Since the vase life of heliconia can be many weeks, Suzi had an idea. Perhaps the florists and hotels would love these flowers. One day she harvested a large bunch of different blooms and went to visit the local hotels and florists. Without exception they remarked that they were indeed unusual flowers, but that their clients wanted roses and carnations and tulips and lilies. They indicated that if their clients ever did ask for some of these strange flowers, they would know whom to contact.

Suzi wasn't happy with their response. One day she was shopping and bought some large vases. She made up some lovely arrangements and decided to pay the hotels another visit. She'd thought about the florists, and decided maybe they didn't like flowers that lasted too long.

Drei oder vier Helikonienarten wuchsen bereits in Australien, bevor wir damit begannen, neue Sorten und Arten einzuführen. Sie waren so gut für unsere Gegend geeignet, dass sie früh und reichlich blüten, viele auch ständig. Sie im Garten zu bewundern ist schön, aber es schien uns auch logisch, die Blüten abzuschneiden und damit das Haus zu schmücken, um sich noch länger daran erfreuen zu können.

Da sich Helikonien in einer Vase für Wochen halten können, hatte Suzi eine Idee: Vielleicht würden Floristen und Hoteliers diese Blüten mögen. Also stellte sie einen großen Bund dieser Blüten zusammen und zeigte ihn den örtlichen Blumenhändlern und Hoteliers. Alle stimmten darin überein, dass dies in der Tat ungewöhnliche Blumen seien, aber sie meinten auch, dass ihre Kunden lieber Rosen, Nelken, Tulpen und Lilien hätten. Dennoch deuteten sie an, das sie ja nun wüssten, wo sie diese fremdartigen Blumen erhalten könnten - falls jemals ein Kunde danach fragen würde.

Suzi war nicht sehr glücklich über diese Reaktionen. Eines Tages kaufte sie einige grosse Vasen und bestückte sie mit wunderschönen Helikonien-sträussen. Sie waren so schön, dass sie beschloss, den Hotels einen weiteren Besuch abzustatten. Sie dachte auch an die Floristen und ihr kam der Gedanke, dass diese vielleicht Blumen nicht mocht-en, die zu lange hielten.

Heliconia orthotricha

Costus productus

Voodoo Lily

Variegate Pineapple

Madagascar flowers

She went to the hotels and offered them a free vase of flowers - no payment required - all she asked for was that the hotel place them on their front counters and listen to what their customers said about them. She left her business card and returned home a little smug. She expected that within a short time they would phone her back and ask for more flowers.

Three weeks went by without a phone call. On the fourth week she finally got a call - but it was from Sydney! Apparently a flight attendant who had seen Suzi's flowers like them so well that she inquired about what they were and who grew them.

When the flight attendant returned to Sydney, she told her florist about the beautiful flowers she had seen in Queensland. The result: Early one morning, Suzi received a phone call from a chap asking, "What the hell is a heliconia?" Suzi tried to describe these bold flowers over the phone, but the florist couldn't visualize them. Suzi ended up sending the florist a sample box. Later that week he phoned back and said that he was in love with those flowers called heliconias. He wondered if he could buy 50 boxes! Twice a week!

We didn't even know where to buy the boxes, but we are quick learners, and by the mid 1980's we had become the largest tropical flower producer in the north.

Sie ging zu den Hotels und bot ihnen jeweils einen kostenlosen Strauss an. Das einzige, worum sie bat, war, dass der Strauß an der Rezeption zu platzieren sei und dass sie, die Mitarbeiter, auf die Reaktionen der Kunden achten sollten. Sie hinterliess ihre Visitenkarte und kehrte selbstzufrieden nach Hause zurück. Sie erwartete innerhalb kürzester Zeit Anrufe mit Nachbestellungen für weitere Blumen.

Drei Wochen vergingen ohne eine einzige Anfrage. In der vierten Woche endlich bekam Suzi einen Anruf - aber er kam aus Sydney. Offensichtlich hatte eine Flugbegleiterin Suzis Blumen gesehen und liebte diese so sehr, dass sie nachforschte, welche Blumen es waren und wer sie züchtete. Nach ihrer Rückkehr in Sydney erzählte die Flugbegleiterin ihrem Blumenhändler von den wunderschönen Blumen, die sie in Queensland gesehen hatte. Die Folge: Dieser rief eines Morgens bei Suzi an und fragte: "was zum Teufel ist eine Helikonie?" Suzi bemühte sich, ihm am Telefon zu beschreiben, was für ausdrucksstarke Blumen das seien, aber er konnte sie sich nicht vorstellen. Also schickte Suzi ihm eine Auswahl zu. Gegen Ende der Woche rief er zurück und erzählte hocherfreut, dass er sich in die Schönheit der Helikonien verliebt habe. Er fragte, ob er 50 Kartons dieser Blumen bestellen könne - zweimal pro Woche!

Wir wussten zuerst nicht einmal, wo wir die vielen Kartons kaufen konnten, haben aber schnell gelernt. Mitte der 80er Jahre waren wir der grösste Produzent tropischer Blüten in Nordaustralien.

Heliconia angusta

Pachira

Backscratcher Ginger

Cordyline

Red Torch Ginger

Between our rows of tropical fruit trees, we cultivated heliconia flowers. Row after row of tropical flowers soon filled our land and the neighboring portion. Then came relatives of the heliconia- the gingers, then calatheas, and so on.

We would wake up at 2:00 am (yes, morning!) and grab our headlamps and go out to cut the blooms. By dawn they were in the shed and being packed. Most of these plants have large leaves, and if the sun comes up and beats down on them, they become stressed, thus shortening the vase life of the flowers. By mid morning they were packed in boxes, driven to the airport, 100 km to the south, and shipped air freight to Sydney, Melbourne, Brisbane, Adelaide and even overseas to Hong Kong and Japan.

We were not marketing professionals and couldn't afford to hire one. We took a chance on the belief that a fresh flower would sell itself, and made it our goal to have our flowers arrive in the shops within 24 hours. The gamble worked! The flower business was successful. It bloomed and bloomed - until 1989.

That year we had a pilot strike in the major airlines. Planes ceased flying. Trucks and trains were too slow. Our flowers suffered too much damage intransit, and soon we couldn't sell them.

Zwischen den Reihen unserer tropischen Obstbäume züchteten wir Helikonien. Reihe um Reihe tropischer Blumen bedeckten schon bald unser Land und die angrenzenden Flächen. Dann kamen die verwandten Arten der Helikonien hinzu, Ingwerarten, Calatheas und so weiter.

Morgens um zwei Uhr (kein Scherz!) standen wir auf, schnappten unsere Stirnlampen, zogen los und schnitten die Blüten. Bei Tagesanbruch waren sie im Schuppen und wurden verpackt. Die meisten dieser Pflanzen haben grosse Blätter. Wenn die Sonne hervorkommt und auf sie niederbrennt, wird die Frische der Pflanzen beeinträchtigt. Dies vermindert ihre Lebenserwartung in der Vase. Noch vormittags waren sie in Kisten verpackt, zum 100 km südlich gelegenen Flughafen gebracht und per Luftfracht nach Sydney, Melbourne, Brisbane, Adelaide und sogar Übersee nach Hongkong und Japan unterwegs.

Wir waren keine Marketingspezialisten und konnten uns auch keine leisten. Wir gaben dem Ganzen eine Chance, weil wir fest daran glaubten, dass eine frische Blume sich praktisch von selbst verkauft. Unser Ziel war es, die Blüten innerhalb von 24 Stunden an die Geschäfte auszuliefern. Die Rechnung ging auf! Das Geschäft mit den Blumen war erfolgreich. Es blüte und blüte - bis 1989.

In jenem Jahr gab es einen Pilotenstreik bei den wichtigsten Fluggesellschaften. Die Flugzeuge blieben am Boden. Lastwagen und Züge waren zu langsam. Unsere Blumen erlitten zuviele Schäden auf dem Transport und wir konnten sie nicht mehr verkaufen.

Caesalpinia

Moth orchid Habenaria sp (Ivory Coast)

Heliconia chartaceae

Beehive ginger

Gloriosa Lily

We thought about the situation. Australia is a vast nation.People live even in the most remote parts - maybe not a lot of people, but some do. We rely on airplanes for our daily life. If our machinery breaks down and it's not a common part, we get the part sent up overnight - by airfreight - so we can get moving again. Some of the cattle and sheep stations are so vast they use planes to round up their cattle and sheep. The Royal Flying Doctor service was created to get medical attention to those out stations and remote communities. We need the airplanes flying.

We were naive in thinking the government wouldn't let the pilot strike last. As large and vast as Australia is, it is one of the most urbanised nations in the world. More than 75% of the population lives in the southeast corner, from Brisbane down to Sydney and across to Melbourne and Adelaide. They live close enough to each other to get most of their goods and services quickly by road or rail. They didn't need the planes.

The pilots strike lasted 6 long months. Many businesses went bankrupt. It was devastating to the rural and tourist economies.

Suzi and Alan decided that being held to ransom by just one sector of the economy was not prudent and decided to wind back the flower business. And as the planes started flying, so too did people, and we started getting visitors - visitors coming to see our collection of plants.

Wir überdachten die Situation. Australien ist ein riesiges Land. Es leben Leute selbst in den entlegensten Winkeln. Flugzeuge sind Teil unseres täglichen Lebens. Geht eine unserer Landmaschinen kaputt und wir benötigen ein spezielles Ersatzteil, wird es über Nacht per Luftfracht hierher geschickt und wir können weiter arbeiten. Einige Rinder- und Schaffarmen sind so riesig, dass sie mit Flugzeugen ihre Herden zusammentreiben. Die "königlichen fliegenden Ärzte" wurden gegründet um die entlegenen Farmen und Kommunen ärztlich zu versorgen. Ganz offensichtlich sind wir recht abhängig von Flugzeugen.

Wir waren so naiv zu glauben, dass die Regierung den Pilotenstreik nicht lange andauern lassen würde. Trotz riesiger Ausdehnungen ist Australien eine der am stärksten verstädterten Nationen der Erde. Mehr als 75% der Bevölkerung lebt im Südosten, zwischen Brisbane und Sydney und weiter zwischen Melbourne und Adelaide. Sie leben dicht genug zusammen, um ihre Waren und Dienstleistungen schnell genug per Strasse oder Bahn zu erhalten. Sie brauchen Flugzeuge nicht wirklich.

Der Pilotenstreik dauerte sechs lange Monate. Viele Geschäfte gingen Pleite. Für die Landwirtschaft und die Tourismusbranche war es verheerend.

Wir erkannten, dass die ökonomische Abhängigkeit von nur einer Einnahmequelle zu riskant war. Wir beschlossen, das Geschäft mit den Blumen zurückzu fahren. Als der Flugverkehr wieder aufgenommen wurde, bekamen wir Besucher. Besucher, die unsere Pflanzensammlung sehen wollten.

Thonningia sanguinea

Hedychium ginger

Medinella scortechnii

Calanthe pulchra

Begonia Madagascar

Some of our visitors were people that we go to the jungles with to learn more about plants. Some are influential, like the Curator of Botany at the Smithsonian Institution, others from Botanical Gardens in North America, Europe and Asia. Most of these people can only grow the plants we collect in glasshouses and they were impressed with the collection we had growing out in the open.

They knew we were trying to change our business and return to the lifestyle that brought us here, and suggested that maybe we should think about turning our place into a botanic garden. We decided to do a trial and let more visitors come. They did come - sometimes alone, or by two's, by the carload or even minibus. We would take them for walks in the garden and admire the flowers, taste the fruits, talk about plants and rainforests, and then retire to our home where we had a cup of tea or coffee and freshly baked pastries.

We enjoyed the visitors and we met some of the nicest people in the world. Many have become our friends. We enjoyed the strolls in the garden, but probably had too many cups of teas and scones. Our only disappointment was that we weren't getting our work done.

We talked to our friends who encouraged us and told them that the time wasn't quite right to establish a botanic garden. We suggested that perhaps we could deed our land so that people could visit after we died. We knew that we had a valuable collection and we wanted people to be able to see it and learn from it, but had too much work to do - too many dreams still to fulfil.

One friend thought that our suggestion was selfish, and we were taken aback. What difference could it possibly make to others if we kept the garden to ourselves during our lifetime? Our friend reminded us that some of the plants we had collected were in fact extinct in the wild, as the forests from which they came were gone forever. He reminded us that we had found plants that were new to science. Our garden contained plants that didn't even have names and plants that had certainly never been cultivated before. We came to the realisation that we were the custodians of some very important plants that people needed to know about. The world could not wait until we died to receive the messages we had found in the rainforests. We could not risk that those messages might be lost or distorted with the passage of time.

Mit einigen unserer Besucher gehen wir in den Dschungel, um ihnen mehr über die Pflanzen beizubringen. Einige sind einflussreich, wie z.B. der Kurator für Botanik des Smithsonian Instituts und andere Mitarbeiter von Botanischen Gärten in Nordamerika, Europa und Asien. Die meisten Besucher können die Pflanzen aus unserer Sammlung nur in Gewächshäusern ziehen und waren von unseren Freilandpflanzungen sehr beeindruckt.

Sie wussten, dass wir versuchten, unsere Geschäftsausrichtung zu ändern, um zu dem Lebensstil zurückzukehren, der uns ursprünglich hierher geführt hatte. Sie schlugen vor, unser Anwesen in einen botanischen Garten zu verwandeln. Wir wollten es ausprobieren und mehr Besucher kommen lassen. Sie kamen - einige alleine, andere zu zweit, mit dem Auto oder gar mit dem Minibus. Wir führten sie auf Rundgänge durch den Garten, sie bewunderten die Blumen, versuchten die Früchte, wir redeten über Pflanzen und den Regenwald. Dann gingen wir zurück zum Haus, tranken Tee oder Kaffee und aßen frisch gebackenen Kuchen.

Wir genossen die Zeit mit den Besuchern und trafen einige der nettesten Leute der Welt. Viele wurden unsere Freunde. Wir genossen die Rundgänge durch den Garten, auch wenn wir möglicherweise zuviel Tee tranken und zuviel Buttergebäck aßen. Der Hauptnachteil aber war, dass wir unsere Arbeit nicht mehr verrichten konnten.

Wir sprachen mit den Freunden darüber, die uns zuvor dazu ermutigt hatten, und sagten ihnen, dass die Zeit vielleicht noch nicht reif sei für einen botanischen Garten. Wir schlugen vor, dass wir unser Land übertragen könnten, damit es nach unserem Tode für die Öffentlichkeit zugänglich würde. Wir waren uns bewusst, dass wir eine wertvolle Sammlung hatten und wünschten uns schon, dass die Leute alles anschauen und davon lernen konnten - wir hatten aber noch zu viel Arbeit und viel zu viele Träume.

Ein Freund fand unseren Vorschlag recht egoistisch und wir waren irritiert. Welchen Unterschied würde es schon für andere machen, wenn wir den Garten während unseres Lebens für uns alleine behielten? Unser Freund erinnerte uns daran, dass einige unserer Pflanzen in der Wildnis bereits ausgestorben seien und dass die Wälder, aus denen sie stammten, für immer verschwunden sind. Ausserdem wies er darauf hin, dass wir Pflanzen gefunden hätten, die für die Wissenschaft neu waren. In unserem Garten wuchsen Pflanzen, die noch nicht einmal einen Namen hatten und sicher auch noch nie gezüchtet wurden. Wir kamen zu der Erkenntnis, dass wir die Wächter einiger sehr wichtiger Pflanzen waren, von denen die Menschen erfahren mussten. Die Welt konnte nicht bis nach unserem Tode warten, um die Botschaft zu erhalten, die wir in den Regenwäldern gefunden hatten. Wir durften nicht riskieren, dass dieses Wissen im Laufe der Zeit verloren ging oder verfälscht wurde.

Educational talk

We were encouraged to join an organization that many other Botanic Gardens are members of - Botanic Gardens Conservation International - based at Kew Gardens in England. We found we embraced their goals and aspirations and shared a commitment to educate people about the importance of saving plants and ecosystems.

We realise that we are just a family, one family, and that maybe our input might not be significant, or earth saving, but we must try to do our bit - try to do something positive for our planet. Our resources are minimal, so we needed to find a way to make the garden self-funding. Tourism is a large business in tropical Queensland and we wondered if perhaps tourists would like what we have and believe in what we are trying to achieve. First we had to set our goals clearly, we wanted to be careful to create something that is manageable, something we enjoy, and something that will allow us to 'live our dreams'.

We settled on three preconditions.

1. To remain private while we are alive, after all, this is our home.
2. To become an educational garden and assist people in learning about plants, and
3. To cater only to groups of people. We surmised that with a group of people, we would know ahead of time when they would visit. With this knowledge, we could make them special guests in our garden and home, while still being able to get our work done. This would mean we would not be "open" all the time for visitors.

Some tourism industry representatives said our plan would never work. Others encouraged us. We formally changed from being a fruit and flower farm to The Botanical Ark in 1990-91, and each year we are getting closer to achieving our goals.

Wir wurden ermutigt, einer Organisation beizutreten, zu der viele Botanische Gärten gehören: der "Botanic Gardens Conservation International", in Kew Gardens, England. Wir fanden uns wieder in deren Zielen und

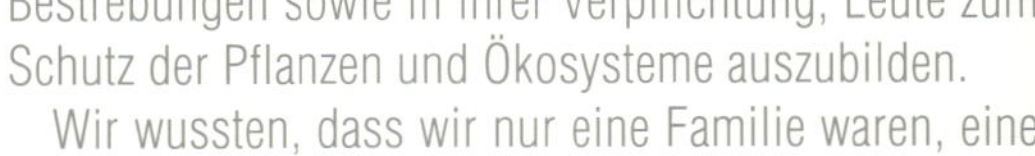
Bestrebungen sowie in ihrer Verpflichtung, Leute zum Schutz der Pflanzen und Ökosysteme auszubilden.

Wir wussten, dass wir nur eine Familie waren, eine einzige Familie, und dass unser Beitrag vielleicht nicht so massgeblich war. Aber wir wollten unser "Quäntchen" dazu beisteuern und versuchen, etwas Positives für unseren Planeten zu tun. Unsere Rücklagen waren gering und wir mussten einen Weg finden, dass sich der Garten selbst tragen würde. Tourismus ist ein grosses Geschäft im tropischen Queensland und wir überlegten, ob Touristen das mögen würden, was wir zu bieten hatten. Und ob sie an das glauben würden, was wir erreichen wollten. Zuerst mussten wir unsere Ziele klar definieren. Wir wollten sorgfältig bei den Vorbereitungen sein, um das Ergebnis gut managen zu können, Spass zu haben und unsere Träume ausleben zu können.

Wir legten drei Voraussetzungen fest:

1. Es sollte privat bleiben, solange wir leben, schliesslich ist es unser Zuhause.
2. Es sollte ein Lehr-/Anschauungsgarten werden und den Leuten helfen, etwas über Pflanzen zu erfahren und
3. Es sollte Mahlzeiten nur für Gruppen geben. Wir nahmen an, dass wir nur bei geschlossenen Gruppen im voraus wissen würden, wann diese zu Besuch kamen. Wir konnten ihnen einen "speziellen" Besuch im Garten und im Haus anbieten und waren nebenbei in der Lage, unsere Arbeit zu erledigen. Dies bedeutete auch, dass wir die Besuchszeiten einschränken konnten.

Einige Tourismusvertreter sagten, das würde so nie funktionieren, andere ermutigten uns. 1990-91 verwandelten wir die Früchte- und Blumenfarm in die "Botanical Ark". Seither kommen wir unseren Zielen jedes Jahr ein Stückchen näher.

Suzi serving Breadfruit chips

The verandah at the Botanical Ark

Ethnobotany

Ethnobotany is the study of plants which are utilised by humans. We decided to design The Botanical Ark gardens around these useful plants as one way of illustrating how valuable rainforests are to all of us.

Timbers, food, medicines, dyes, fibers, oils, resins, waxes, tools, musical instruments and clothing are just some of the products we obtain from rain forests. We actually pay money for these resources, so we can clearly see the economic benefits of preserving their source.

Try, for a moment, to think of a rainforest product that is important in your life. Perhaps a favorite nut or wood; perhaps a lifesaving medicine. We often take what we have for granted and rarely think about the origin of our bounty.

Die Ethno-Botanik ist das Studium von Nutzpflanzen. Wir entschlossen uns, die Botanical Ark ganz auf Nutzpflanzen hin auszurichten, um zu betonen, wie wertvoll der Regenwald für uns alle ist.

Holz, Nahrungsmittel, Medikamente, Kosmetik, Farbstoffe, Fasern, Öl, Harze, Wachse, Werkzeuge, Musikinstrumente, Kleidung sind nur einige Dinge, die wir vom Regenwald erhalten. Wir bezahlen ja tatsächlich auch Geld dafür und können so ganz klar erkennen, welchen wirtschaftlichen Nutzen es hat, diese Quellen zu schützen.

Versuchen Sie mal einen Moment an Pflanzen zu denken, die aus dem Regenwald kommen und eine wichtige Rolle in Ihrem Leben spielen. Vielleicht an bevorzugte Nüsse oder Holz, vielleicht an eine lebensrettende Medizin. Zu oft nehmen wir Dinge, die wir nutzen, als selbstverständlich hin und machen uns keine Gedanken über deren Herkunft.

Professor Ake Assi and Alan

Medicinal plants / Ivory Coast

Rubber

Lets look at rubber. It is a product from the rubber tree Hevea brasiliensis, found wild in the Amazon basin, and now one of the most cultivated trees throughout the tropical world. Rubber assists us in transportation, by providing us with the tyres of our motor vehicles. It may also be part of the floor mats, window seals, and if it rains, those valuable windscreen wipers. If you play golf, it is probably the - centres of your golf-balls, at the beach or out on the reef it may be part of the mask, fins and snorkels. There is no need to mention what rubber is used for at night, so we're sure you agree that it is a very valuable commodity.

Had you been able to visit the Amazon 200 years ago, you may have passed by rubber trees without ever imagining their future potential. Can you imagine your life now without rubber?

One of the interesting aspects of our natural world is that the more we observe, study and experiment, the more we discover. And the more it can benefit us.

Lassen Sie uns doch mal Gummi etwas näher betrachten. Gummi ist ein Produkt des Hevea Brasiliensis Baumes. Der kommt vor allem im Amazonasbecken vor und zählt heute zu den Bäumen, die in den Tropen am häufigsten angepflanzt werden. Bei Fahrzeugen beispielsweise gibt es für Gummi vielfältige Anwendungsmöglichkeiten. Er ist Rohstoff für Reifen, kann Teil der Teppiche sein und findet sich auch in Fensterdichtungen und Scheibenwischern wieder.

Beim Golfspielen ist das Innere Ihres Golfballs wahrscheinlich aus Gummi, beim Schwimmen und Schnorcheln vermutlich auch ein Teil Ihrer Taucher-maske, der Flossen und des Schnorchels. Selbst wenn wir hier nicht weiter ausführen wollen, wozu der Gummi des Nachts verwendet wird, stimmen Sie sicher zu, dass Gummi ein wertvoller Gebrauchsartikel ist.

Hätten Sie die Möglichkeit gehabt, vor 200 Jahren das Amazonasgebiet zu besuchen, wären Sie sicher an den Gummibäumen vorbeigelaufen, ohne sich auch nur im geringsten deren zukünftiger Bedeutung bewusst zu werden. Können Sie sich aber heute noch ein Leben ohne Gummi vorstellen?

Eine der interessantesten Eigenschaften unserer natürlichen Umgebung besteht darin, dass wir, je mehr wir sie beobachten, studieren und mit ihr experimentieren, umso mehr Neues in ihr entdecken - und Nutzen aus ihr ziehen.

Tapping rubber

Rubber tyres / Maroantsetra / Madagascar

Kepple Apple

Back in the 1970s we met a chap from Florida, Bill Whitman, who was one of the founders of the Rare Fruit Council International. Bill told us that there was a fruit from Indonesia called the Keppel Apple that, upon consumption, would make all one's bodily odours and excretions smell like violets. Bill was a mentor to us and his recommendations were usually worth following up.

The Keppel Apple sounded like an interesting fruit that might benefit people, so we headed to Indonesia and searched from island to island until we found it. A seed was planted and seven years later we had our first fruit.

The 3 cm roundish brown fruit doesn't look very exciting, and its taste takes a little getting used to, and the first fruit left no noticeable improvement in body odour. Perhaps Bill had got it wrong. The following year we had a good crop of fruit, and we decided to conduct an experiment. Three of us each ate a few fruits and worked hard all day long. At the end of the day we all noticed an appreciable improvement in body odour. It worked! Apparently the volatile compounds in the flesh of the fruit travel our metabolic pathways and are released through our sweat glands (and other places). And the more we sweated, the more it worked.

Maybe someday a clever biochemist will study plants like these and we can benefit in the form of a deodorant that is not only safe to use, but nutritious as well. But only if we still have the plants to study.

1970 trafen wir einen Bekannten aus Florida, Bill Whitman, der auch einer der Gründerväter des "Rare Fruit Council International" war. Bill erzählte uns, dass es in Indonesien eine Frucht mit dem Namen "Kepple Apple" gäbe, nach deren Genuss jedermanns Ausdünstungen nach Veilchen duften würden. Bill war für uns ein Mentor und normalerweise waren seine Empfehlungen und Vorschläge es wert, dass man sie weiter verfolgte.

Der Keppel Apple schien eine interessante Frucht zu sein, die den Leuten helfen würde, und so machten wir uns auf den Weg nach Indonesien. Wir durchforschten eine Insel nach der anderen, bis wir die Frucht gefunden hatten. Wir pflanzten einen der Samen und sieben Jahre später ernteten wir die ersten Früchte.

Die 3 cm großen, runden, braunen Früchte sehen nicht sehr aufregend aus und an ihren Geschmack muss man sich erst gewöhnen. Der Genuss erster Früchte führte zu keiner nennenswerten Verbesserung des Körpergeruchs. Vielleicht hatte sich Bill ja geirrt. Im folgenden Jahr hatten wir eine gute Ernte und entschlossen uns zu einem Experiment. Drei von uns aßen einige der Früchte und arbeiteten den ganzen Tag lang hart. Zum Tagesende stellten wir alle eine beachtliche Verbesserung unserer Körperausdünstungen fest. Es funktionierte! Scheinbar wanderten die flüchtigen Bestandteile des Fruchtfleisches durch unseren Stoffwechsel und wurden über die Schweissdrüsen freigesetzt. Je mehr wir schwitzten, desto besser funktionierte es.

Vielleicht wird dies eines Tages ein cleverer Biochemiker erkennen und ein Deodorant entwickeln, das nicht nur sicher in der Anwendung, sondern darüberhinaus auch nahrhaft ist. Aber natürlich nur, wenn es diese Pflanzen dann noch gibt.

Different varieties of chilis

Keppel Apple

Annato

Have you ever seen photos of the indigenous Amazonian Indians with a red paint covering their bodies? Maybe you have actually met some of these people. The body paint they utilise is one of the most important colourings of the modern world. It comes from a plant called 'Achiote' - Bixa orellana, and produces the colouring we know as 'annato' or E160(b).

This shrub from Amazonia provides a colouring that is odourless, tasteless, water soluble and non-toxic. It colours some of our cosmetics, it makes our butter and margarine yellow, our pastries golden and is even used in some beers and ice creams. Some poultry farmers mix it in their foods so the yolks will come out a darker colour, and some zoos have actually used it to keep their flamingos pink, when the natural diet wasn't available.

Annato is used in up to 500 different products that we humans consume every day.

Haben Sie je Aufnahmen der eingeborenen Amazonasindianer mit ihren roten Körperbemalungen gesehen? Vielleicht haben Sie sie sogar selbst kennengelernt. Die Körperfarbe, die sie einsetzen, enthält einen der wichtigsten Farbstoffe der heutigen Welt. Er stammt von einer Pflanze mit dem Namen "Achiote"-Bixa orellana. Sie liefert einen Farbstoff, den wir als "Annato" oder auch E160 (b) kennen.

Dieser Busch vom Amazonas liefert uns einen Farbstoff, der geruchlos, geschmacklos, wasserlöslich und ungiftig ist. Er färbt einige unserer Kosmetikartikel, macht Butter und Margarine gelber, unser Backwerk goldfarben und wird sogar einigen Biersorten und Eiscremes zugesetzt. Einige Hühnerzüchter mischen ihn dem Hühnerfutter bei, damit das Eigelb eine dunklere Farbe bekommt. Zoologische Gärten füttern ihn manchmal sogar ihren Flamingos, damit diese pinkfarben bleiben, was ohne ihre natürliche Nahrung sonst nicht der Fall wäre.

Annato wird heute in über 500 Produkten des täglichen Lebens eingesetzt.

Bixa orellana

Annatoo colouring

Ginger

At the Botanical Ark, we grow and research plants. We are not doctors, nor pharmacists, so we do not supply or recommend treatments. We leave it to our visitors to do their own research in investigating how other cultures handle their ailments. Although you may be amazed at the simplicity and potential benefits of natural medicines, it is always necessary and important to seek professional advice.

Ginger is one of the most important spices and flavourings we use today - Ginger beer, ginger biscuits, crystallized ginger, gingerbread, even ginger tea. Ginger has long been an item of commerce and was traded over vast distances due to the root´s ability to grow after long dormant periods.

But how many people realise that ginger is one of the most used medicines in the world today? Almost two-thirds of the population of the planet are in Asia and the sub-continent of India, and most know the remedial and curative properties that ginger has.

Ginger is known to be effective in preventing and treating nausea caused by motion and morning sickness. It improves blood circulation, relieves gas build-ups and indigestion, and relieves bacterial infections and muscle spasms. It has also been used (often in traditional mixtures) for the treatment of asthma, burns, coughs and colds, diarrhoea, dysentery, jaundice, mumps, nasal block, piles and smallpox. As with all things we ingest or apply, it is very important to know the correct dosages and preparations, and to determine if allergies or complications exist.

Ingwer zählt heutzutage zu den wichtigsten Gewürzen bzw. Geschmacksrichtungen: Ingwerbier, Ingwerbiskuits, kristallisierter Ingwer, Ingwerbrot, sogar Ingwertee. Ingwer ist seit langem eine Handelsware und konnte auch schon früher über weite Entfernungen verschickt werden, da die Wurzeln lange Zeit keimfähig bleiben.

Aber wer weiß schon in unserem Kulturkreis, dass Ingwer heute eines der am häufigsten verwendeten Medikamente ist? In Asien und Indien aber, wo zwei Drittel aller Menschen leben, kennen viele die heilenden Wirkungen des Ingwers.

Ingwer ist bekannt für seine Wirksamkeit zur Vorbeugung und bei der Behandlung von Übelkeit (auch bei Schwangerschaft) und Antriebsschwäche. Er verbessert die Blutzirkulation, hilft bei Blähungen und Magenbeschwerden, lindert bakterielle Infektionen sowie Muskelkrämpfe. Er wurde auch (oft in traditionellen Zusammensetzungen) für die Behandlung von Asthma, Verbrennungen, Husten und Erkältungen, Durchfall, Ruhr, Gelbsucht, Mumps, Nasenverstopfung, Hämorrhoiden und Pocken eingesetzt. Wie mit allen Dingen, die wir einnehmen oder anwenden, ist es auch hier sehr wichtig, die richtige Dosierung und das richtige Präparat einzusetzen und abzuklären, ob Allergien oder sonstige Komplikationen vorliegen.

Auf der Botanical Ark züchten und erforschen wir Pflanzen. Aber wir sind keine Ärzte oder Apotheker und können daher keine Behandlungen anbieten oder empfehlen. Wir überlassen es unseren Besuchern, selbst nachzuforschen, wie andere Kulturen Krankheiten heilen. Obwohl Sie überrascht sein werden, wie einfach und doch wirkungsvoll viele dieser Naturheilverfahren sind, ist es immer notwendig und wichtig, professionellen Rat einzuholen.

Ginger flowers

Ginger of commerce

Costus

Trekkers in the jungles of Asia, Africa and the Americas will almost certainly pass by plants in the Costus family. These spiral plants that are related to ginger typically occur in the understory. They produce colourful flowers and bracts to attract their pollinators.

The Botanical Ark has a large collection of costus and while observing their growth and pollination, Alan happened to eat one of the flowers. It was exciting, both in its substance and flavour. The ever-cautious Suzi was reluctant to try it – and who could blame her? Twice before she had taken Alan to the hospital suffering the adverse effects of eating plants that weren't really edible. Suzi pleaded not to let the children have them or eat any more until he researched it further .A literature search was performed, and I contacted my colleagues who knew about costus, including some who lived in the forests where costus grew. A year passed and still no confirmation was received that anyone has ever eaten the flowers. Not one to let a year pass by without results, Alan ate several more flowers. Each one tasted nice, and the telltale signs of poisoning - like rashes, vomiting, shortness of breath, blurred vision, faintness or Montezuma's Revenge - evaded him.

It seemed as if Alan may be onto something new. More research was conducted and it was determined there were no poisons, and the flowers were indeed edible. Alan eagerly commenced sampling the numerous species that grew in the garden. They came in all colours, shapes and sizes - from white to pink, red, yellow, orange, green, purple, and even different flavours - some tasted like lemons, some like strawberries! After confirming these results with colleagues, Alan published his observations and today many chefs in the tropics serve costus flowers in their meals. Lunch or dinner at the Botanical Ark is not complete without the colourful costus flower salad. Research did uncover numerous uses of the costus plants. Some stems are beaten flat and used in making matting, the juice from the stems of one species from the Amazon is used to treat earaches, and in India, they utilise the roots of another as a contraceptive.

The assumption that we know so much about our environment can be called into question when we realize that even common plants can yield new products.

Bei Trecks durch die Dschungel von Asien, Afrika und Amerika trifft man unweigerlich auf Pflanzen der Costus-Familie. Normalerweise kommen diese, mit dem Ingwer verwandten Pflanzen, im Unterholz vor und haben farbenfrohe Blüten, um ihre Bestäuber anzulocken.

Die Botanical Ark hat eine stattliche Costus-Sammlung. Eines Tages ass ich aus einer Laune heraus eine der Blüten. In ihrer Konsistenz wie auch im Geschmack war sie eine leckere Überraschung. Die stets vorsichtige Suzi traute sich nicht zu kosten. Wer konnte ihr das verdenken? Hatte sie mich doch schon zwei Mal ins Krankenhaus gebracht, nachdem ich Früchte probiert hatte, die nicht wirklich essbar waren. Suzi bat mich, die Kinder da herauszuhalten und keine weiteren Blüten mehr zu essen, bevor ich sie nicht genauer erforscht hatte. Ich zog Fachliteratur zu Rate und fragte Kollegen und Freunde, die in jenen Wäldern leben, wo Costus Arten vorkommen. Selbst nach einem Jahr gab es keine Bestätigung, dass irgend jemand diese Blumen je gegessen hätte. Nicht, dass die Zeit ungenutzt verstrichen wären - ich probierte zwischenzeitlich weitere Blüten. Jede schmeckte vorzüglich und die Anzeichen einer Vergiftung, wie Ausschläge, Erbrechen, Atemnot, Haluzinationen, Bewusstlosigkeit oder Montezumas Rache stellten sich nicht ein.

Es schien so, als hätte ich etwas Neues entdeckt. Weitere Forschungen ergaben, dass die Blüten ungiftig und von daher tatsächlich essbar waren. Eifrig versuchte ich weitere Blüten unserer zahlreichen Arten. Sie wuchsen in allen erdenklichen Farben, Formen und Grössen. Es gab sie in weiß, lila, rot, gelb, orange, grün und violett, einige schmeckten wie Zitronen, andere wie Erdbeeren! Nachderm Kollegen die Ergebnisse bestätigt hatten, veröffentlichte ich die Entdeckung. Seitdem servieren viele Köche in den Tropen die Blüten zu ihren Gerichten und keine Mahlzeit auf der Botanical Ark ist ohne Costus-Blütensalat komplett. Costuspflanzen sind aber auch noch für andere Dinge sehr nützlich. Die Stengel kann man flach klopfen und daraus Matten flechten, der Saft aus dem Stengel einer anderen Art vom Amazonas hilft bei Ohrenschmerzen und in Indien verwendet man die Wurzeln einer weiteren Art zur Empfängnisverhütung.

Die leichtfertige Annahme, dass wir über unsere Umwelt gut Bescheid wüssten, gerät ins Wanken, wenn uns auch heute noch eine ganz gewöhnliche Pflanze neue Produkte bescheren kann.

Costus flower

Costus flowers for salads

Explorations

Travelling to some of the remote corners of the world is an assurance of interesting times. As the years pass by some memories get a little fuzzy around the edges, but not all. Each trip has special moments, some good, some bad, some absolutely terrifying, and some so very special.

Often just getting to a place can be eventful...

Here's a story, told by Alan, of the time he and a colleague had a mishap leaving a rather small, but lovely Central African country: We were told that the President's daughter needed to fly somewhere the following day on the one plane that was the "National Airline." This meant that the once-a-week flight scheduled for tomorrow would be pre-empted, and we would fly out a day early (today!). Apparently, such schedule changes were not unusual.

We had just arrived from a trip into the south west and fortunately were able to scramble to the airport to catch the plane - leaving 20 kg (44 lb) of wet laundry behind. We boarded and of course the plane was almost empty- everyone else was waiting for the scheduled departure tomorrow- well almost everyone.

There were about 10 of us seated towards the rear of the plane when a rather large man came in and sat in the first class seats in front. While we were preparing for takeoff and going through the safety procedures, the flight attendant asked to see the man's boarding pass.

Reisen in die entlegenen Ecken der Welt sind ein Garant für interessante Zeiten. Einige Erinnerungen verschwimmen mit der Zeit, aber längst nicht alle. Jede Reise hat ihre speziellen Momente, gute, schlechte, ein paar fürchterliche und einige ganz besondere.

Hier ist die Geschichte eines Zwischenfalles, der mir und einem Kollegen beim Verlassen eines kleinen, liebenswerten Landes in Zentralafrika widerfuhr. Uns wurde gesagt, dass die Tochter des Präsidenten am nächsten Tag mit "unserem" Flugzeug verreisen wolle, das die gesamte "Staatliche Fluggesellschaft" des Landes darstellte. Das bedeutete für uns, dass der wöchentliche Flug von morgen einen Tag vorgezogen wurde, also auf heute! Offensichtlich waren solche Flugplanänderungen dort gar nicht so ungewöhnlich.

Wir kamen gerade von einer Exkursion in den Südwesten zurück und konnten glücklicherweise rechtzeitig zum Flughafen hasten, um den Flug gerade noch zu erreichen, ließen aber in der Eile 20 kg nasser Wäsche zurück. Wir stiegen ein und natürlich war das Flugzeug fast leer - alle warteten auf den planmäßigen Abflug am nächsten Tag. Na ja, fast alle...

Im hinteren Teil des Flugzeuges hatten sich schon etwa zehn Passagiere eingefunden, als ein grosser Mann hereinkam und sich vorne in die erste Klasse setzte. Während wir die Sicherheitshinweise durchgingen und uns auf den Start vorbereiteten, fragte der Flugbegleiter den Mann nach seinem Ticket.

Tracking in the jungle

Exploration trips into the unknown

As they spoke a language unfamiliar to us, I can only assume the following: He confirmed the man was in the wrong section and should go sit in his assigned seat in the rear of the plane. An argument ensued and the flight attendant departed. He returned with his colleagues determined to get the man to move. Still the passenger refused, and the argument got steamier. He rose as if to beat his chest and question their authority. A priest from the rear of the plane came forward and tried to calm things down and resolve the situation. He failed too. The pilot attempted to assert some authority - he couldn't and left.

The now more than irate passenger got up and moved towards the door. The mood in the plane was elation until he stormed forward through the cockpit door and a scuffle broke out. The plane jerked, and bumped and thumped and the shouting level became more frenetic. Eventually the man returned to 'his' first class seat.

Airport security guards entered the plane and tried to remove the man, but were unsuccessful. They left and it seemed like the hours passed in the steamy body of this aircraft going nowhere when, suddenly, armed military personnel stormed the plane from the rear and the front and forcibly removed the impediment to our travel.

We were on our way - to another African country, where at the international airport, the lights didn't work, the toilets obviously hadn't worked for quite some time, and nobody wanted you to leave - not without supplying them with a substantial gift.

Da sie sich in einer uns unbekannten Sprache unterhielten, kann ich fogendes nur vermuten: Er stellte fest, dass der Mann in der falschen Klasse saß und forderte ihn auf, zu seinem rechtmäßigen Sitz im hinteren Teil der Maschine zu gehen. Ein Wort gab das andere und der Flugbegleiter verschwand. Er kam mit seinen Kollegen zurück, wild entschlossen, den Mann zum Umzug zu bewegen. Aber der Passagier weigerte sich und der Streit wurde hitziger. Er plusterte sich auf und stellte die Zuständigkeit des Flugbegleiters in Frage. Ein Priester aus dem hinteren Teil des Flugzeugs ging nach vorn. Er versuchte zu schlichten und das Problem zu lösen. Auch er scheiterte. Sogar der Pilot versuchte vergeblich seine Autorität zur Geltung zu bringen und zog wieder ab.

Bridging

Mittlerweile war der Passagier sehr zornige stand auf und ging zur Tür. Die schlechte Stimmung im Flugzeug wich großer Erleichterung - leider nur sehr kurz. Der aufgebrachte Passagier stürmte durch die Cockpittür und ein Handgemenge kam in Gang. Das Flugzeug wackelte und ruckelte, während das Geschrei geradezu frenetisch wurde. Schließlich kehrte der Mann auf "seinen" Platz in der ersten Klasse zurück.

Sicherheitspersonal vom Flughafen eilte herbei und versuchte, den Mann herauszuzerren - ohne Erfolg. Sie verschwanden und es schien, als vergingen Stunden im schwülheissen Rumpf der Maschine, ohne jegliche Lösungsaussicht, als plötzlich bewaffnete Soldaten von hinten und vorne die Maschine stürmten, um - diesmal erfolgreich - das Starthindernis unseres Fluges zu entfernen.

Endlich waren wir auf dem Weg in ein weiteres afrikanisches Land, in dessen internationalem Flughafen die Lichter nicht funktionierten, die Toiletten offensichtlich seit geraumer Zeit nicht in Betrieb waren und uns niemand gehen lassen wollte - ohne vorher ein großzügiges "Geschenk" von uns bekommen zu haben.

Treehouse for canopy scientific research (Costa Rica)

... and the Korup Road:

For the past few days it had rained incessantly in Korup, possibly the wettest place in Africa, We had walked through the mud and swollen creeks oblivious to the fact that the only road out was rapidly becoming unpassable. When our time exploring these incredible forests was up, we began to contemplate our situation. It was still raining hard when we departed.

The road to Ekondo Titi wasn't too bad - perhaps the rumours we heard in Mundemba were wrong - that the road was washed out. It kept raining, and the road got muddier, and more slippery. Paul was an experienced driver who had survived the roads of Congo (Zaire) for the past few decades. He managed to get our 4 wheel drive past numerous bogged vehicles and up hills where groups of young men waited to assist less fortunate vehicles or drivers. We smiled. We shouldn't have. The road had a soil mix from the nearby volcanic Mount Cameroon. Even on the flat road we were sliding and the holes were getting deeper. On one of the hills we couldn't slide forward and negotiated a price for getting pushed up. Many hills lay ahead. As we approached a small village on the top of a hill, a drinks truck blocked the road. The only way past was on the top of a steep bank to the left. We smugly negotiated this tricky route only to hit a 'toll' just before the top. We had to pay for a log bridge across the ditch onto the road.

... und dann die Strasse nach Korup:

Seit Tagen hatte es in Korup, dem wahrscheinlich feuchtesten Flecken Afrikas, praktisch ununterbrochen geregnet. Wir kämpften uns durch Schlamm und angeschwollene Bäche ohne dass uns bewusst wurde, dass auch die einzige Strasse für den Rückweg schnell unpassierbar wurde. Erst als unsere Expedition durch diesen ungeheuer schönen Regenwald zu Ende ging, begannen wir, uns über unsere Situation sorgen zu machen. Bei unseren Aufbruch regnete es noch immer heftig.

Die Straße nach Ekondo Titi war gar nicht so übel. Vielleicht waren die Gerüchte, die wir in Mundemba gehört hatten, einfach falsch: Die Straße sei weggespült! Aber es regnete weiter und die Strasse wurde zunehmend matschiger und rutschiger. Paul war ein erfahrener Fahrer. Seit Jahrzehnten hatte er die Straßen des Kongo (Zaire) gemeistert. Es gelang ihm, unser Allradfahrzeug an unzähligen steckengebliebenen Autos vorbei zu manövrieren und Steigungen zu bezwingen, an denen Gruppen junger Männer auf weniger glückliche Fahrer oder Autos hofften, um ihnen - gegen Bezahlung - weiterzuhelfen. Wir belächelten die Unglücklichen - was wohl etwas voreilig war. Die Strassenoberfläche bestand aus einem schlüpfrigen Erdgemisch des nahegelegenen vulkanischen "Mount Cameroon". Selbst auf den flachen Streckenabschnitten rutschten wir und die Schlaglöcher wurden tiefer. An einem der nächsten Hügel kamen wir nicht mehr weiter und mussten nun selbst Preise aushandeln, um hinaufgeschoben zu werden. Leider lagen noch sehr viele Hügel vor uns.

Prof. Ake Assi & Alan

Blocked road (Ivory Coast)

Pushers (Cameroon)

Road from Mundemba

Road from Mundemba / Cameroon

Everywhere we had to stop because of bogged vehicles or gangs of pushers, we noticed that intense negotiations were going on, and that we were indirectly part of it. Arguments were presented that if they did not let those in front pass for free, there would be no revenue from us or others that may follow. Eventually compromises were made and we edged forward.

We slid into the right ditch and our truck was now at 45 degrees and at least one wheel was airborne. We were stuck. The Negotiations started with, "We are poor people in Africa. We are hungry and starving," (not really), and ended with the promise to get us up the steep hill for a moderate sum. It was hard work pushing, with no assistance from the tyres or engine. At the top we discovered another flat tyre - another payment. The last 5 km had taken us more than 5 hours!

Als wir uns einem kleinen Dorf auf einer Anhöhe näherten, blockierte ein Getränkelaster die Strasse. Der einzige Weg daran vorbei führte über eine steile Böschung zur Linken. Selbstzufrieden verhandelten wir die "Maut" für diese schwierige Strecke, nur um kurz darauf, noch vor dem Scheitelpunkt der Anhöhe, nochmals abkassiert zu werden. Diesmal galt der Wegzoll einer Brücke aus Baumstämmen, die zurück auf die Strasse führte.

Vegetable stall / Ivory Coast

Überall mussten wir wegen steckengebliebener Fahrzeuge oder Banden von "Schiebern" anhalten. Es gab intensive Verhandlungen, in die wir ganz unfreiwillig verwickelt wurden. Würde man sie nicht umsonst passieren lassen, argumentierten Vorausfahrende, gäbe es auch keine Einkünfte von uns oder anderen, die nachfolgten. Kompromisse wurden geschlossen und wir zuckelten weiter.

Dann rutschten wir in den rechten Strassengraben, das Auto neigte sich um 45 Grad und zumindest ein Reifen hing frei in der Luft. Wir steckten fest. Die Verhandlungen begannen mit "wir sind arme Leute hier in Afrika", "wir leiden und sind am verhungern" (nicht wirklich!) und endeten mit dem Versprechen, uns gegen Überreichung einer kleinen Summe den steilen Hügel hinaufzuschieben. Es war harte Arbeit, das Auto aus dem Graben heraus zu bekommen. Oben auf dem Hügel angekommen, registrierten wir einen platten Reifen - die nächste Zahlung wurde fällig. Für die lezten 5 km hatten wir über fünf Stunden benötigt!

Sassandra river / Tai National Park / Ivory Coast

Our arrival at Atalavia (Madagascar) was memorable. That morning the bay of Angontil was peaceful, except for the few passing rain showers. The humpback whales that tried to fly the afternoon had gone somewhere else to play. The coastline was rainforests from the cloud shrouded mountains to the sea except when long stretches of golden sands brightened the scenery. The sun managed to coerce the clouds away from the beach as we landed. We waded from the boat to the beach through the kind of water that seems to only appear in magic holidays and dreams.

The fan shaped crowns of 'travellers palms' rose above the forest and waved us a welcome. A local lady greeted us at the beach and as we set up camp she brought us fresh fruit, warm cassava and smiling children. Settling in was easy, but it was the forest we wished to explore. The next morning we set off as the sun rose to light our path. We followed the creek as it rose into the mountains, having to cross it a few times as the only way in was blocked by steep terrain. For the next 6 hours we climbed ridge after ridge, only to go down and up over and over again until we found yet another ridge to climb. The forest was quiet, with the distant creek a murmuring exception in the background.

Occasionally a group of lemurs would pass through the trees overhead, and maybe stop to wonder why we were taking the more difficult track. The giant buttress roots of Canari trees had to be climbed over and around as we trekked into a still steeper forest. We reached a place where the creek divided and the boulders grew to an enormous size, and the moss and orchids and ferns carpeted the rocks and the trunks of the trees. Something happened, and we still aren't sure what or how or why, but there are places inside the forests where magic occurs, and all the plants are lovely and different -where the leaves are blue, or spotted or crinkled, or velvet or patterned. A striped mongoose scurried between the rocks. Birds came to see who was 'here' and a musky fragrance warmed the air.

Unsere Ankuft in Atalavia (Madagaskar) ist uns noch heute in bester Erinnerung. Friedvoll lag an jenem Morgen die Bucht von Angontil vor uns. Nur ein paar Regenschauer zogen vorbei. Die Buckelwale, die sonst nachmittags hier sprangen, hatten sich wohl einen anderen Spielplatz gesucht. Der Regenwald erstreckte sich entlang der Küste von den wolkenverhangenen Berghängen bis hinab zum Meer, unterbrochen nur von langen, goldfarbenen Sandstränden. Gerade als wir anlegten, gelang es der Sonne, die Wolken vom Strand zu vertreiben. Vom Boot zum Strand wateten wir durch jene Art von zauberhaftem Wasser, das es eigentlich nur in Reisekatalogen oder Träumen gibt.

Die fächerförmigen Kronen der "Bäume der Reisenden" reckten sich über dem Regenwald empor und winkten uns ein herzliches Willkommen herüber. Eine einheimische Frau begrüsste uns am Strand, und während wir unser Zelt aufbauten, brachte sie uns frisches Obst, warmen Cassave und lächelnde Kinder. Sich hier niederzulassen, wäre ein Leichtes gewesen, aber wir waren ja gekommen um den Regenwald zu erforschen. Am nächsten Morgen brachen wir auf, als die Morgensonne unseren Weg gerade ein wenig erhellte. Wir folgten dem Fluss aufwärts in das Gebirge und mussten ihn einige Male überqueren, da das steile Gelände uns den Weg versperrte. Für die nächsten sechs Stunden überkletterten wir Bergrücken um Bergrücken, nur um immer wieder erneut hinunter zu steigen bis zum nächsten Bergkamm, der wiederum zu erklimmen war. Der Wald war still, nur der Bach gurgelte sanft im Hintergrund.

Gelegentlich zog eine Gruppe Lemuren über uns durch die Bäume, um nur kurz innezuhalten und sich zu wundern, warum wir wohl den beschwerlicheren Weg da unten gewählt hatten. Die riesigen Stützwurzeln der Canari Bäume mussten auf unserem Weg in den zunehmend steileren Wald überklettert oder umgangen werden. Wir erreichten eine Stelle, an der sich der Fluss verzweigte und die mächtigen Felsen noch an Grösse zunahmen. Die Baumstämme und Gesteinsbrocken waren dicht mit Moos, Orchideen und Farnen überwachsen. Etwas geschah und wir wissen bis heute nicht was, wie oder warum - aber es gibt Orte im Wald, wo magische Dinge geschehen, wo alle Pflanzen so anders und bezaubernd aussehen, wo die Blätter blau, gesprenkelt oder geknittert vielleicht auch samtig oder gemustert sind. Eine Streifen-Mongoose huschte zwischen die Felsen. Vögel kamen, um nachzusehen wer wohl da war und Moschusduft erfüllte die Luft.

Antalavia river / Madagascar

Magical Forest / Masoala Peninsula / Madagascar

There are times when you can recognise that magic moment, maybe it was when all the hairs on my body stood on end, or maybe when I walked through the wall of warm air, or maybe when I no longer felt the pain in my aching heels. Whenever it was, I knew it. Sometimes one can look for years without finding these places, I now believe they find us, not the other way around.

Our worst fears are meeting people with guns, like the time we arrived in Guatemala during a revolution, and had to lie on the streets as bullets passed by, or when a corrupt drug squad policeman in Colombia wouldn't believe I was only interested in fruits and that the white powder was indeed foot powder.

Our greatest joys are visiting those wild places and meeting the face of nature, like when I was on a small tributary in the very western part of the Brazilian Amazon. We were paddling our canoe up one of the back rivers, when a white dolphin surfaced and swam along side us for half an hour. Or waking up in the morning on a mountain where all the valleys are clouds and the mountain-tops islands of serenity. Especially enjoyable is meeting people who appreciate and respect their rainforests.

Staying with local villagers who are so eager to share their home and meagre belongings with us and teach us all about their lives is so rewarding. It encourages us to use their knowledge as a way to teach others.

Es gibt Zeiten, da kann man diese magischen Momente leicht erkennen. Vielleicht war es damals, als sich all meine Körperhaare aufstellten, oder als ich durch eine Wand warmer Luft schritt, vielleicht auch als ich den Schmerz in meiner Ferse nicht länger spürte. Wann immer es geschah, ich wusste es. Manchmal kann man jahrelang suchen, ohne diese Orte zu finden. Ich glaube inzwischen, dass die Orte uns finden, und nicht umgekehrt.

Unsere grösste Sorge ist es seit jeher, auf bewaffnete Leute zu treffen. Wie damals, als wir während einer Revolution in Guatemala eintrafen und flach auf der Strasse lagen, während Kugeln über unsere Köpfe flogen. Oder als mir ein korrupter Drogenpolizist in Kolumbien nicht glauben wollte, dass ich nur an Früchten interessiert sei und dass das weiße Pulver tatsächlich nur Fusspuder war.

Unsere grösste Freude hingegen ist es, immer wieder unberührte Orte zu entdecken und ergreifende Begegnungen mit der Natur zu erleben. Wie beispielsweise an einem kleinen Nebenfluss im westlichsten Teil des brasilianischen Amazonas. Wir paddelten mit unserem Kanu einen Seitenarm stromaufwärts, als ein weißer Flussdelphin auftauchte und uns freudig eine halbe Stunde lang begleitete. Tief berührt hatte es uns auch, als wir früh morgens auf einem Berggipfel aufwachten, um den herum die Wolken wie Täler und die Bergspitzen wie Inseln des Friedens wirkten. Auch ist es immer wieder erfreulich, Menschen zu treffen, die ihren Regenwald zu schätzen wissen und ihn respektieren.

Hochinteressant wird es , wenn Dorfbewohner, die darauf bestehen ihr Heim und ihre kärgliche Habe mit uns zu teilen, über ihr Leben erzählen. Es ermutigt uns, ihr Wissen zu nutzen und an andere weiterzugeben.

Airport at Antalaha after a cyclone (Madagascar)

Provisioning for trip to Masoala / Madagascar

Araca Sorbet

Araca Sorbet

500ml (2 cups) araca pulp
625ml (2.5 cups) sugar syrup
2 egg whites (small or 1 large)

Sugar syrup:
625ml (2.5 cups) sugar
500ml (2 cups) water

In a saucepan bring sugar and water to the boil. Stir to dissolve sugar and simmer until it thickens slightly. Cool and refrigerate.

Araca pulp:
Remove skin, deseed, blend and sieve. Mix syrup and pulp and pour into ice cream machine and turn on. Put egg whites in a stainless steel bowl and place bowl over a steaming pot of water. Whisk until ribbon stage and pour into sorbet mixture and churn until frozen. Place into freezer over night.

Zuckersirup:
Bringen sie Zucker und Wasser in einem Kochtopf zum Kochen. Den Zucker unter Umrühren auflösen und solange köcheln, bis die Flüssigkeit leicht dicklich wird. Abkühlen lassen und gefrieren.

Araca Fruchtfleisch:
Haut entfernen, entkernen, mixen und durch ein Sieb drücken. Sirup und Fruchtfleisch mixen, in die Eiscrememaschine schütten und einschalten. Eiweiss in eine Edelstahlschüssel geben und auf einen Topf mit kochendem Wasser stellen. Mit dem Schneebesen zähflüssig aber nicht ganz steif schlagen und dem Sorbetgemisch beigeben. Schlagen, bis es gefroren ist. Über Nacht in den Kühlschrank stellen.

Aracá sorbet

Araca Juice

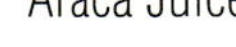

Araca Juice

4-5 medium sized araca fruit
250ml (1 cup) water
sugar syrup
ice

Sugar syrup:
125ml (1/2 cup) sugar dissolved in
125 ml (1/2 cup) boiling water

Remove skin and de-seed araca fruits. Place pulp and water into blender with cooled sugar syrup. Add ice and blend until smooth. Adjust amount of water and sugar to taste. Serve over ice and garnish with fresh mint.

Die Haut entfernen und die Araca-Früchte entkernen. Geben Sie das Fruchtfleisch, das Wasser und den kalten Zuckersirup in den Mixer. Eis hinzugeben. Zu einer cremigen Konsistenz mixen. Mit Wasser und Zucker abschmecken. Mit Eis und etwas frischer Minze servieren

Green papaya salad

Pomelo Salad
with fresh Prawns and coconut lime dressing

Coconut lime dressing

Pomelo Salad with fresh prawns and coconut lime dressing

Serves about 6 persons
1 pink pomelo
1 white pomelo
2 ripe avocados
1kg ((2.2lb) red papaya (or other sweet one)
1 cucumber
1/2 kg (1.1 lb) fresh cooked prawns
1 nice lettuce

Wash lettuce and line 6 individual serving bowls with leaves. Skin pomelo, remove white pith and seeds, being careful to keep the segments intact. Peel and de-seed the avocados and cut into thick slices. Do the same for the papaya and cucumber. The cucumber should be sliced lengthwise. Peel and de-vein prawns. Arrange all the above on top of the lettuce in the bowls and drizzle with a little of the coconut lime dressing. Garnish with snow pea sprouts or fresh mint. Serve chilled.

Den Kopfsalat waschen und sechs Servierschüsseln mit den Blättern auslegen. Die Pomelo schälen, die weisse Haut und die Kerne vorsichtig entfernen, sodass die einzelnen Segmente unversehrt bleiben. Die Avocados schälen, entkernen und in dicke Scheiben schneiden. Mit den Papayas ebenso verfahren. Die Gurke der Länge nach schneiden. Krabben schälen und ausnehmen. Alles auf den Salatblätter in den Schüsseln anrichten und etwas Coconut Lime Dressing darüber träufeln. Mit chinesischen Erbsensprossen oder frischer Minze garnieren. Gekühlt servieren.

Pomelo

Coconut lime dressing

250ml (1 cup) coconut milk
1 tblsp lime juice
1 teasp fish sauce
2 teasp sugar
1 teasp chopped red chilli

Combine all ingredients and mix well.

Alle Zutaten zusammenschütten und gut durchmixen.

Pomelo salad

Cassava Rosti
with Mango Salsa

Sweet Potato, Taro & Cassava

Cassava Rosti

1 litre (4 cups) grated fresh cassava
190 gms (3/4 cups) chopped eschalots
1 teasp salt
1 tblsp water

Peel young cassava roots and remove centre core. Grate (or use food processor) and place in large bowl. Mix in eschalots, salt and water. Shape into small patties and fry in hot oil. When bottom is browned, flip whole cake(s) over and fry other side. When cooked turn out onto serving platter and serve with mango salsa or chilli sauce.

Junge Cassava schälen und den Kern aus der Mitte entfernen. Raspeln (oder mit der Küchenmaschine zerkleinern) und in eine große Schüssel geben. Schalotten, Salz und Wasser beimischen. In mehrere kleine Küchlein formen und in heißem Öl backen. Wenn die Unterseite gebräunt ist, umdrehen und die andere Seite backen. Die fertigen Röstis mit Mangosalsa oder Chilisauce servieren.

Mango Salsa

125ml (1/2) cup diced mango
125 ml (1/2) cup seeded and diced tomato
1 tblsp. red onion finely chopped
30ml (1/8) cup shredded fresh mint
1 teasp. extra virgin olive oil
1 tblsp. lime juice
1 teasp. balsamic vinegar
1/2 teasp. fresh ground sea salt
1/3 teasp. fresh ground black pepper

Gently toss all ingredients

Alle Bestandteile vorsichtig vermischen.

Cassava rosti

Sweet Potato, Taro and Cassava

Sweet Potato, Taro and Cassava are very important root vegetables and are easily grown in the tropics. They are all very high in carbohydrates and are easily used as you would use an ordinary white potato.
Boiled and mashed they make nice patties, sliced and deep fried delicious chips, and are especially tasty roasted.

Süsskartoffeln, Taro und Cassava sind sehr wichtige Wurzelgemüse, die in den Tropen gut gedeihen. Sie sind reich an Kohlenhydraten und können ähnlich wie gewöhnliche weisse Kartoffeln verwendet werden. Sehr gut schmecken sie gebraten oder gekocht. Zerstampft sind sie gut geeignet für Bratlinge, in dünne Scheiben geschnitten und fritiert ergeben sie leckere Chips, und geröstet sind sie besonders wohlschmeckend.

Tropical tubers kaukau, cassava, taro

Pumpkin Curry

Pumpkin Curry

Enough for 4-6 persons
1 litre (4 cups) pumpkin
250 gms (1/2 lb) green beans
2 tblsp peanut oil
1-2 teasp red curry paste
2 tblsp ginger grated
2 cloves garlic
2 stalks lemon grass - lower tender white portion only
1 slice fresh galangal (laos) chopped
75mm (3 in) fresh tumeric grated
12 curry leaves
1 chilli - remove seeds
3 kaffir lime leaves
2 saw tooth coriander leaves
2 tblsp palm sugar
2 tblsp fish sauce
1 tblsp lime juice
125ml (1/2 cup) fresh basil leaves
1-1.25 l. (4-5 cups) coconut milk

Prepare pumpkin by removing skin and seeds. Cut pumpkin into bite size chunks (around 25mm (1 in)). Top and tail and wash green beans. Place ginger, garlic, chopped lemon grass, chopped galangal, tumeric, curry leaves, chilli, kaffir lime leaves and coriander into a blender and add a bit of oil to help blend. Blend to a smooth paste. In a wok or saucepan heat the oil. When hot, add the curry paste and fry being careful not to burn it. Then add the ingredients from the blender and stir, frying for around 2 minutes.

Gradually add the coconut milk stirring, to blend. Add the pumpkin and cook until just about soft. Then add the green beans, palm sugar, lime juice and fish sauce. Simmer until vegetables are just cooked. Before serving add the fresh basil leaves. Serve with jasmine rice.

Kürbis schälen, Kerne entfernen und in mundgerechte Stücke schneiden. Grüne Bohnen waschen und die Enden abscheiden. Geben Sie Ingwer, Knoblauch, zerkleinertes Zitronengras, zerkleinertes Galangal, Tumeric, Curryblätter, Chili, Kaffir-Limeblätter und Koriander in einen Mixer und fügen Sie etwas Öl hinzu, um es zu einer schön glatten, cremigen Paste zu mixen. In einem Wok oder einer Kasserolle Öl erhitzen. Wenn heiss, Currypaste hinzugeben und vorsichtig anbraten (brennt leicht an!). Dann die Paste aus dem Mixer dazugeben, umrühren und noch ca. 2 Minuten braten.

Kokosmilch unter ständigem Umrühren langsam hinzugeben. Die Kürbisstücke hineingeben und kochen bis sie fast weich sind. Dann die grünen Bohnen, Palmzucker, Limonensaft und Fischsauce hinzugeben. Köcheln lassen, bis das Gemüse fast gar ist. Erst direkt vor dem Servieren frisches Basilikum dazugeben. Passt gut zu Jasmin-Reis.

Pumpkin curry

Curry ingredients

Breadfruit Gnocchi

with Ricotta and Spinach and fresh Tomato Sauce

Breadfruit Gnocchi
with Ricotta and Spinach and fresh Tomato Sauce

250 gms (1/2 lb) green breadfruit (mature but still firm)
125 gms (1/4 lb) fresh spinach - stems removed, well washed
90 gms (3oz) ricotta cheese
30 gms (1oz) fresh grated parmesan
1 egg
1/8 teasp fresh grated nutmeg
1/2 teasp salt
1/8 teasp freshly ground black pepper
100 gms (3.5 oz) plain flour

Place spinach in pan without water except for the drops still clinging to the leaves after washing. Cover and steam until tender. Remove, drain and cool. Wring out as much water as possible and chop very finely. Remove skin and core of the breadfruit and boil until very soft, drain and dry. While breadfruit is still warm mash finely. In a large bowl combine breadfruit, spinach, ricotta, parmesan, egg, nutmeg, salt and pepper. Add flour gradually to form a dough. Don't overwork it. On a lightly floured surface form gnocchi into a rope about 1.5cm (3/4 inch) thick. Slice into 1.5cm pieces. Roll each piece into a ball. Hold dough ball between thumb and forefinger, pushing thumb into dough. Bring 5 litres (8 pints) of water to boil add 1.5 extra teasp salt. Slide gnocchi into the boiling water and stir gently. When they float to the surface scoop out and leave to drain. Transfer to serving dish. Pour the fresh tomato sauce over gnocchi. Scatter shaved or grated parmesan cheese over the top and serve.

Spinat nach dem Waschen abtropfen lassen und ohne zusätzliches Wasser in eine Pfanne geben. Abdecken und gar dünsten. Abgießen und abkühlen lassen. Möglichst viel Wasser auswringen und sehr klein schneiden. Die Breadfruit schälen und entkernen, sehr weich kochen, abgießen und trocknen lassen. Die noch warme Breadfruit fein pürieren. Die Breadfruit zusammen mit dem Spinat, sowie Ricotta, Parmesan, Ei, Muskatnuss, Salz und Zucker in eine große Schüssel geben und durchmengen. Langsam Mehl hinzugeben, bis ein Teig entsteht. Nicht zu stark kneten. Die Masse auf einer leicht bemehlten Fläche zunächst zu einem Strang von 1,5 cm Stärke formen. In Stücke von 1,5 cm Länge schneiden. Jedes Gnocchi zu einer Kugel rollen, das Teigbällchen zwischen Daumen und Zeigefinger halten und den Daumen in den Teig drücken. 5 Liter Wasser mit 1,5 Teelöffel Salz zum Kochen bringen. Die Gnocchis ins kochende Wasser geben und leicht umrühren. Wenn sie an die Oberfläche steigen, herausnehmen und abtropfen lassen. Auf die Servierteller geben und mit der frischen Tomatensauce übergiessen. Mit geriebenem Parmesankäse bestreuen und servieren.

Tomato Sauce

75ml (1/8 pint) extra virgin olive oil
6 garlic cloves chopped finely
1/2 small onion finely diced
2 tbsp flat leaf parsley or
8 large basil leaves
1.25kg (2 lb 9oz) fresh ripe tomatoes, peeled, de-seeded and coarsely chopped.
1/2 teasp salt
fresh ground black pepper to taste.

Heat the olive oil on medium-low heat, add the garlic, onion and parsley. Sauté until onion softens. Add the tomatoes and salt, using a potato masher to break the tomatoes up. Raise the heat and simmer (about 20 minutes) stirring occasionally to reduce. Add pepper, and if using basil, shred finely and add just before serving.

Olivenöl auf kleiner Flamme erhitzen, Knoblauch, Zwiebeln und Petersilie hinzu geben. Rösten, bis die Zwiebeln weich werden. Tomaten und Salz hinzugeben. Die Tomaten mit einem Kartoffelstampfer zerdrücken. Temperatur anheben und etwa 20 Minuten köcheln lassen, gelegentlich umrühren, um Anbrennen zu verhindern. Pfeffer und feingehacktes Basilikum erst kurz vor dem Servieren darüber streuen.

Breadfruit gnocchi

Green Breadfruit on the boil

Mamey Sapote Milkshake

Mamey Sapote Milkshake

500ml (2 cups) mamey sapote pulp
1 litre (4 cups) soy milk (GM free)
250m (1 cup) vanilla ice cream (optional)
1/4 teasp freshly grated nutmeg
ice

Place all ingredients in blender and blend until smooth. Serve garnished with a slice of fruit and grated nutmeg.

Alle Zutaten in einen Mixer geben und cremig mixen. Mit einer Scheibe Obst und gemahlenem Muskat garnieren.

Mamey Sapote Pie

Mamey Sapote Pie

500ml (2 cups) mamey sapote pulp
1 pinch of salt
375ml (1.5 cup) coconut cream
3 egg yolks
1 whole egg
85ml (1/3 cup) brown sugar
1 teasp grated fresh ginger
1 teasp cinnamon
1/3 teasp ground ginger
1/3 teasp nutmeg
1/4 teasp ground cloves
1 pastry shell (25cm (10in)

Place all ingredients (except pastry) in the blender and mix well. Pour into unbaked pastry shell. Bake at 200C (400F) for 10 minutes. Lower temperature to 140C (275F) for 30 minutes. Remove and cool. Glaze with heated honey or maple syrup. Serve sliced with a small amount of whipped cream and some shaved or grated chocolate.

Alle Zutaten (ausser der Teigtasche) in einen Mixer geben, gut durchmixen und in die ungebackene Teigtasche schütten. Bei 200 Grad C für 10 Minuten backen. Die Temperatur auf 140 Grad C senken und 30 Minuten weiterbacken. Aus dem Ofen nehmen und abkühlen lassen. Mit heissem Honig oder Ahornsirup glasieren. Die Einzelportionen mit etwas Schlagsahne und geschabter Schokolade garniert servieren.

Mamey con leche

Mamey sapote pie

Guanabana Dacquiri

Guanabana Dacquiri

100ml (4oz) guanabana pureed
30ml (1oz) Bacardi rum
30ml (1oz) sugar syrup (30gms sugar in 30ml water)
1 tblsp fresh lemon or lime juice
ice

Place all ingredients in blender and blend until smooth. Garnish with sliced rambutan or another colourful tropical fruit.

Alle Zutaten mit einem Mixer zu einer cremiger Konsistenz schlagen. Mit einer aufgeschnittenen Rambutan oder einer anderen farbenfrohen, tropischen Frucht garnieren.

Guanabana Cheesecake with Passionfruit

Guanabana Cheesecake
with Passionfruit

CRUST:
175 gms (6 oz) sweet biscuits, crumbed
pinch of cinnamon and nutmeg
75 gms (3 oz) melted butter

Mix crust ingredients together and press mixture into greased pie dish and bake unfilled for about 7 mins. at 180C (375F)

Guanabana Dacquiri

Alle Tortenbodenzutaten vermischen und in eine eingefettete Kuchenform geben. Etwa 7 min bei 180 Grad C backen.

FILLING:
250 gms (1 cup) cream cheese, at room temperature
400 gms (14oz) condensed milk
85ml (1/3 cup) fresh lemon juice
250ml (1 cup) pureed guanabana pulp
3 teasp. gelatine
65ml (1/4) cup hot water
2-3 fresh passionfruit

Beat cream cheese until smooth. Slowly add condensed milk while beating. Add lemon juice and pureed guanabana, beat well.

Sprinkle gelatine over 65ml (1/4 cup) hot water and beat well until dissolved. When cool add gelatine mixture to other ingredients and mix well. Pour into pie shell and set in fridge. (Can also be frozen). To serve, top with plenty of passionfruit.

Frischkäse zu cremiger Konsistenz schlagen. Unter ständigem Schlagen langsam Kondensmilch hinzugeben. Zitronensaft und pürierte Guanabana unterheben und gut durchschlagen.

Gelatine in 65 ml heissem Wasser auflösen und dabei gut rühren. Die abgekühlte Gelatine gleichmäßig in die Masse unterrühren. Auf den Tortenboden geben und in den Kühlschrank stellen (lässt sich gut einfrieren). Vor dem Servieren großzügig mit Passionsfrucht dekorieren..

Guanabana cheescake with Passionfruit

Champadek Fritters

Macadamia Ice Cream

Macadamia Ice Cream

5 egg yolks
200ml (4/5 cup) cream
100ml (2/5 cup) milk
100ml (2/5 cup) coconut cream
1 vanilla pod
85ml (1/3cup) castor sugar
125ml (1/2cup) macadamia nuts chopped

In a saucepan, infuse split vanilla pod with cream, milk, and coconut cream. Gently heat but don't boil. In another bowl whisk yolks and sugar. Slowly pour cream mix into yolks and sugar whisking all the time. Return to saucepan on low heat. Stir with wooden spoon until mixture coats the back of the spoon. Cool and chill. Place in ice cream machine. Stir nuts through just before freezing.

Champadek Fritters

1 champadek or soft-fleshed jackfruit
flour
oil for deep frying batter

Batter:
1 egg
250ml 1(cup) milk
190ml (3/4 cup) self raising flour
pinch of salt

Beat these ingredients together until smooth.

Remove pulp from around the seeds of a ripe champadek or jackfruit. Dip segments of pulp into flour and then into batter and deep fry in hot oil until golden. Drain and place on paper towel to absorb the oil. Serve hot with ice cream or cream. Optional - while hot roll in a mixture of sugar and cinnamon or freshly grated coconut.

Alle Bestandteile zu einem Teig glattrühren.

Die Kerne vom Fruchtfleisch einer reifen Champadek oder Jackfruit entfernen. Die Fruchtstücke in Mehl wälzen und anschliessend in den Teig tauchen. In siedendem Öl goldgelb fritieren. Abtropfen lassen und auf Papiertücher legen, die das Öl aufnehmen. Heiß mit Eiscreme oder Sahne servieren. Oder - noch heiss - in einer Mischung aus Zucker und Zimt rollen oder frisch geraspelter Kokosnuss rollen.

Ripe Champadek and edible seeds

Gespaltene Vanilleschoten in einem Kochtopf mit Sahne, Milch und Kokosnusspaste übergiessen. Vorsichtig erwärmen, aber nicht kochen. In einer anderen Schüssel mit dem Schneebesen Eigelb und Zucker verrühren. Die Crememischung langsam mit dem Schneebesen dem Eigelb mit Zucker unterheben, dabei immer rühren. Bei kleiner Flamme wieder zurück in den Kochtopf geben. Mit einem Holzlöffel rühren, bis die Masse auch an der Rückseite des Löffels anhängt. Abkühlen und kalt stellen. In die Eiscrememaschine geben und kurz vor dem Gefrierpunkt die gehackten Nüsse unterrühren.

Champadek fritters and Macademia icecream

Conservation

Many of the world's leading biologists believe we are now in one of the mass extinctions that occasionally frequent the earth. Their estimates of the rate of loss of different species of plants and animals may be 50 to 100 species each and every day! The painful truth is that it is the human species that is accelerating this loss.

It was a news report of a lecture that Dr. Peter Raven, Director of the Missouri Botanic Garden, gave to a group in Australia, back in the 1980's that made us finally take notice of what was happening around us. At the time he said we would probably lose 20% of the life on earth in the next 25 years. If you really think about this statement, you must begin to wonder what it might mean for us - not only as individuals, but as a species.

We discussed this claim, and wondered if maybe the newspaper made a mistake. The more we researched, the more confirmations we heard. The earth is indeed in trouble. And it needs help from all of us.

How does an individual, a family or even a classroom of students make any difference? The enormity and gravity of the situation seems insurmountable. If we believe in the individual, and in the belief of individual thought and subsequent actions, then each one of us has the power to change. And collectively we can initiate bigger change.

Viele führende Biologen der Welt glauben, dass wir uns zur Zeit in einer jener Phasen grossen Artensterbens befinden, wie sie die Erde gelegentlich erlebt. Sie schätzen den Verlust an Pflanzen- und Tierarten auf etwa 50-100 pro Tag - jeden Tag! Die traurige Wahrheit ist, dass die menschliche Rasse den Artenverlust so dramatisch beschleunigt.

Letztendlich war es ein Zeitungsartikel über einen Vortrag, den Dr. Peter Raven, Direktor des Missouri Botanic Garden, in den 80er Jahren vor einer Gruppe Australier hielt, der uns bewusst machte, was um uns herum geschah. Er sagte damals, dass wir auf der Erde wahrscheinlich innerhalb der nächsten 25 Jahre 20 % aller Arten verlieren würden. Wenn man sich das einmal vor Augen führt, muss man doch ins Grübeln kommen, was das für uns, nicht nur als Individuen, sondern auch als Spezies bedeutet.

Wir diskutierten diese Aussage und fragten uns, ob die Zeitung vielleicht einen Fehler gemacht hatte. Aber je mehr wir nachforschten, desto mehr Bestätigungen bekamen wir. Die Erde ist wirklich in Schwierigkeiten. Und sie braucht von uns allen Hilfe.

Kann da der Einzelne, eine Familie oder selbst eine Schulklasse überhaupt etwas ausrichten? Die Größe und Schwere dieses Problems scheint unüberwindlich. Wenn wir jedoch an den Einzelnen und die Kraft seiner Ideen und Taten glauben, dann hat jeder von uns die Möglichkeit, etwas zu ändern. Und alle zusammen können wir so einen Umschwung bewirken.

Nutrient recycling

Monte Verde National Park / Costa Rica

One thing is certain, if we sit back and wait for others to make the changes for us, they will never happen.

We wondered how best we might help effect a change, and assist in saving some of the natural wealth of this incredible planet. Our family had no money, no political clout, no friends in high places. Yet we were determined to try and do something.

One of things that impressed us in the arguments re: the pros and cons of development for development's sake was that the defenders of the environment had no vested interests in protecting our natural places. They championed the smallest of spiders and the largest of trees, the driest of deserts and the rivers that ran free. On the other hand, the developers were often motivated by profit only. They had everything to gain by hiding or distorting the truth and maligning the 'greenies'.

Our office door has long been adorned by a now-yellowed clipping from a Sierra Club journal. It reads "Not Blind Opposition to Progress - Opposition to Blind Progress." These were the words of the Sierra Club's first executive director, the late David Brower, with whom we shared a common commitment to protect and preserve the earth.

Eins ist sicher, wenn wir uns zurücklehnen und darauf warten, dass andere für uns das Ruder herumreissen, wird nichts geschehen.

Wir fragten uns, wie wir selbst eine Änderung zum Guten herbeiführen und dazu beitragen könnten, einige der natürlichen Schätze dieses wundervollen Planeten zu retten. Unsere Familie hatte kein Geld, keinen politischen Einfluss und keine Freunde in wichtigen Positionen. Aber wir waren entschlossen, es zumindest zu versuchen.

Saved from dinner ?

Eine Sache, die uns bei den Diskussionen des Für und Wider von Wachstum um des Wachstums Willen überraschte war, dass die Umweltschützer kein wirklich aufrichtiges Interesse am Schutz unserer unberührten Natur zeigten. Sie setzten sich zum Beispiel lieber für die kleinsten Spinnen oder die grössten Bäume, die trockensten Wüsten oder frei laufende Flüsse ein. Und auf der anderen Seite hatten wir die Stadtentwickler, deren oft einzige Motivation die Gewinnmaximierung war. Dies erreichten sie am einfachsten durch Verschweigen oder Verbiegen der Wahrheit und der Verleumdung unserer Grünzonen, den "Greenies".

Unsere Bürotür ziert seit langem ein inzwischen angegilbter Ausschnitt aus einem Sierra Club Journal. Darauf heisst es: "Keine blinde Opposition gegen Fortschritt - aber Opposition gegen blinden Fortschritt". Dies sind die Worte des ersten Geschäftsführers des Sierra Clubs, David Brower. Mit ihm verbindet uns die Selbstverpflichtung, die Erde zu schützen und zu erhalten.

Logging trucks / almost everywhere

We thought about our friends whose ancestors lived in the jungles for thousands of years without destroying it. We thought about our friends from the jungles whose lives were changing as development encroached and the forest disappeared. Over the years we noticed that their children were missing out on some of the valuable knowledge that enabled their relatives to survive. As the forest ebbed into the distance, the ability to teach the skills slipped away too. Their tools, their resources, their ties to the land were being lost.

Much of the tropical forest loss comes as the forests are chopped down and burned for agriculture. We began to equate the burning of these forests with the burning of the world's great libraries and museums. The losses for the human race are incalculable. And these losses are continuous. It is estimated that we lose a football field of rainforest every seven seconds. Some researchers say that figure is far too conservative.

We believed if we could understand the reasons people chop down the forest, we might be able to determine the best ways to help prevent it.

Wir dachten an unsere Freunde, deren Vorfahren seit Jahrtausenden in den Regenwäldern lebten, ohne diese zu zerstören. Wir dachten auch an unsere Freunde im Dschungel, deren Leben sich unter den Beeinträchtigungen durch die Landentwicklung und das Verschwinden der Wälder verändert. Mit den Jahren bemerkten wir, dass ihre Kinder schon einige der wertvollen Kenntnisse verloren hatten, die ihren Verwandten das Überleben sicherten. So, wie der Wald aus ihrem Leben verschwand, kam auch die Fähigkeit, ihnen das Wissen zu vermitteln, abhanden. Ihre Werkzeuge, ihre Schätze und die tiefe Verbundenheit mit ihrem Land gingen verloren.

Ein Grossteil des tropischen Waldes wird der Nutzung tropischer Hölzer und der Brandrodung für die Landwirtschaft geopfert. Wir verglichen die Brandrodung des Regenwaldes mit der Brandstiftung einigen der grossen Bibliotheken und Museen dieser Welt. Der Verlust für die Menschheit ist in beiden Fällen kaum zu beziffern. Und die Verluste gehen weiter. Schätzungsweise alle sieben Sekunden geht eine Regenwaldfläche in der Grösse eines Fußballfeldes verloren. Einige Forscher sagen, dass dieser Vergleich noch viel zu moderat sei. Unserer Überzeugung nach, kann ein Ausweg nur gefunden werden, wenn wir die Gründe verstehen, weshalb die Menschen den Wald abholzen.

Charcoal production

Forest devastation

Two reasons consistently appeared in most of our investigations - too much greed and too many people. The explanations offered for clearing the forest seem noble: "to feed our people" and "to earn a living." Of why they clear it, seems at first to be for 'noble' reasons: "To feed our people"; "to earn a living".

It is difficult to counter these arguments, and we did not feel we had the right to tell people how many children they could or couldn't have. We didn't think we'd get far telling them not to earn a living either. How would we feel being told to go back and live in a cave or the crowded cities from where many came?

We needed to provide a positive reason for people to want to save the forests. The first thought that came to mind was because it supports so much life. It has been said that up to 60% of all of the land based organisms on the planet live in the rainforests, which occupy a little more than just 6% of the planet. That is a good reason. And what about all the oxygen they produce? Without it we would be in strife. And what about the climate moderating benefits? Would global warming accelerate without the forests? Would the sea levels rise faster? Most projections point to a worsening situation, including more severe droughts, exceptional rains and floods and increasing velocity in wind storms.

Zwei Gründe tauchten bei unseren Nachforschungen immer wieder auf: zu viel Habgier und zu viele Menschen. Und oft erscheinen die Erklärungen, warum der Wald gerodet wird, ganz plausibel: "um unsere Leute zu ernähren", "um ein Einkommen zu haben".

Es ist schwierig, diesen Argumenten zu widersprechen. Wir glaubten auch nicht, dass wir das Recht hatten, diesen Menschen vorzuschreiben, wieviele Kinder sie haben oder nicht haben sollten. Und wir glauben erst recht nicht daran, dass es half, ihnen ihren Lebensunterhalt streitig zu machen. Denn wie würden wir uns wohl fühlen, wenn jemand uns vorschriebe, wieder in einer Höhle oder einer der überfüllten Städte zu leben, aus denen viele von uns geflohen sind?

Wir mussten den Leuten gute Gründe geben, damit auch sie den Regenwald retten wollten. Der erste Grund, der uns in den Sinn kam, war der, dass er soviel Leben spendet. Es wurde festgestellt, dass der Regenwald bis zu 60 % aller Landorganismen unseres Planeten beherbergt, dabei aber nur etwas mehr als 6% der Erdoberfläche bedeckt. Das ist doch ein guter Grund. Und was ist mit all dem Sauerstoff, den die Regenwälder produzieren? Ohne diesen wären wir ganz schön in Schwierigkeiten. Und was ist mit den ausgleichenden Einflüssen auf unser Klima? Würde sich die globale Erwärmung ohne die Wälder vielleicht beschleunigen? Würde der Meeresspiegel schneller ansteigen? Alle Berechnungen weisen auf eine Verschlechterung der Situation hin, mit noch mehr schwerwiegenden Dürreperioden, sintflutartigen Regenfällen, Überschwemmungen und einer Zunahme der Windgeschwindigkeiten bei Stürmen.

His future ?

Left to rot !

The latest research indicates climate change is accelerating at a faster rate than imagined. Yet we cannot see the sea levels rising, nor feel the oxygen depletion or the carbon dioxide increasing. How can we expect forest dwellers to change when even we find it hard to quantify these changes. They have no proof. There has to be another way to affect change.

Perhaps asking the forest dwellers to stop clearing when we sit comfortably in our cosy homes, is the wrong approach. Maybe we need to look at the bigger picture and look at who ultimately consumes many of these resources. We thought that if we could prove to people that the forest is more valuable left standing than it is chopped down, perhaps we could make a difference.

We decided maybe we could assist people in recognising these values of a rainforest by designing our garden around those plants that produce items that we actually pay money for. We would target the consumers, the decision makers, the business men and women and the educators. Our message, then, may just flow on to families and co-workers and peers and eventually through to the political system. We had to try.

Die letzten Forschungsergebnisse zeigen, dass die globale Erwärmung schneller voranschreitet als erwartet. Noch können wir den Anstieg des Meeresspiegels nicht sehen. Noch spüren wir nicht, wie sich der Sauerstoffgehalt in der Luft vermindert und der des Kohlendioxids erhöht. Wie können wir dann von den Waldbewohnern erwarten etwas zu verändern, wenn wir nicht einmal selbst in der Lage sind, diese Veränderungen zu quantifizieren. Sie haben keinen "Beweis". Es muss einen anderen Weg geben um Veränderungen einzuleiten.

Die Waldbewohner aufzufordern, das Roden der Wälder einzustellen, während wir in unseren gemütlichen Häusern sitzen, ist wohl der falsche Ansatz. Vielleicht sollten wir die Sache mal mit etwas mehr Abstand betrachten und prüfen, wer denn tatsächlich die meisten der Ressourcen verbraucht. Wir dachten, wenn wir den Leuten beweisen könnten, dass der intakte Wald wertvoller ist als der abgeholzte, könnten wir vielleicht etwas verbessern.

Wir entschlossen uns dazu, die Menschen dabei zu unterstützen, den Wert des Regenwaldes zu erkennen, indem wir unseren eigenen Garten um bestehende Pflanzen und Bäume herum gestalteten, die Dinge liefern, für die wir normalerweise Geld bezahlen. Wir würden damit die Verbraucher, die Geschäftsleute und Lehrer ansprechen. Unsere Botschaft würde dann über deren Familien, Kollegen und Freunde weitergetragen werden und schliesslich auch das politische System erreichen. Wir müssen es versuchen.

Lemur / Nosy Mangabe / Madagascar

Coastal forest / northeast Madagascar

To illustrate the concept, we imagined: What if our financial resources or material assets (our house and land - for you this may be different assets) were tied to the health of the forest? If we managed that forest sustainably, we could get interest, whether it was in the form of new building materials, foods or medicines or money, that would be just fine.

But what if we did not manage it effectively, what if we took more than the forest could sustain, or what if we damaged or destroyed the forest? Eventually someone has to pay to correct the imbalance. We can pass the deficit on to our children and they, their's - but the loss just increases and the interest compounds.

Um das Konzept, das wir meinen, zu verdeutlichen: Was wäre, wenn unsere finanziellen Mittel oder unser materieller Besitz (unser Haus und das Grundstück, für Sie mag es etwas anderes sein) eng mit der Gesundheit des Waldes verknüpft wären? Nur wenn wir diesen Wald nachhaltig schützten, erhielten wir Zinsen, sei es in Form von neuem Baumaterial, Nahrung, Medizin oder Geld. Das wäre erstrebenswert.

Aber was wäre dann, wenn wir den Wald nicht effektiv managen würden, wenn wir mehr wegnähmen, als er uns geben kann? Oder was wäre, wenn wir den Wald beschädigen oder gar zerstören würden? Irgend jemand muss letztendlich den Preis für das gestörte Gleichgewicht bezahlen. Natürlich können wir die Schulden an unsere Kinder weiterreichen und diese wieder an die ihren - aber der Schuldenberg wächst und Zinsen und Zinseszinsen addieren sich auf.

Python

Coastal forest / northeast Madagascar

Quarantine matters!

The movement of seeds and plants around the world has provided people with the basic resources to create incredible cuisines. Try contemplating Italian food without tomatoes, Indian food without chilli and the Irish or Swedes without their potatoes.

Yet the movement of plants has also created havoc where weeds, pests and diseases have invaded natural ecosystems and croplands. Native plant and animal species have disappeared during these invasions, and the cost to the community for control measures can be immense.

Australia, once set free in the Gondwana break-up, developed a unique fauna and flora over many millions of years. Australia has been surrounded by vast oceans, a natural barrier to many of the world's major pests, diseases and weeds until comparatively recent times.

The Botanical Ark is acutely aware of the risks and benefits of introductions of new plant species to our shores. So too, is the Australian Government. We work together in a shared responsibility to try and prevent negative impacts. We have developed what are considered to be some of the most stringent and researched conditions on plant quarantine anywhere in the world.

Quarantine is more than an issue here at The Botanical Ark, it is a way of life.

Der weltweite Austausch von Samen und Pflanzen hat interessierte Menschen mit den Grundlagen für die Zubereitung einer unglaublichen Vielfalt internationaler Gerichte versorgt. Versuchen Sie mal, sich die italienische Küche ohne Tomaten, indisches Essen ohne Chili und die Iren oder Schweden ohne ihre Kartoffeln vorzustellen.

Aber die Pflanzentransporte haben leider auch Chaos verursacht, dort wo fremde Unkräuter, Schädlinge und Krankheiten in natürliche Ökosysteme und Anbauflächen eindrangen. Einheimische Pflanzen und Tierarten verschwanden, und der Kostenaufwand der Kommunen für Ausgleichsmaßnahmen kann immens sein.

Australien ist seit Urzeiten von Ozeanen umgeben, die bis vor vergleichsweise kurzer Zeit eine natürliche Barriere gegen Plagen, Krankheiten und auch Schädlinge darstellten.

Die Botanical Ark, wie auch die australische Regierung, sind sich der Risiken und Vorteile sehr wohl bewusst, die mit der Einführung neuer Planzenarten in unser Land verbunden sind. In unserer gemeinsamen Verantwortung arbeiten wir eng zusammen, um negative Einflüsse zu verhindern. Wir haben die weltweit wohl strengsten Quarantänebestimmungen für Pflanzen erforscht und entwickelt.

Quarantäne ist auf der Botanical Ark mehr als nur ein Thema, es ist ein Bestandteil unseres Lebens.

Blue-winged Kookaburra

Light gaps in an Australian rainforest

Mount Cameroon / Cameroon

Antalavia river / Madagascar

Sassandra river / Tai National Park / Ivory Coast

Rara Avis / Costa Rica

Ankasa Forest Reserve / Ghana

One of the questions we never want to be asked by our children or grandchildren is 'how could you let all those animals and plants go extinct? Weren't they important? What did they do wrong?'

We've already had elders tell us how the now dead drain was once a crystal clear creek where one could see every grain of sand sparkle, even from the deepest holes. And how fish used to swim in these creeks. And how birds used to stalk and catch the fish, often from a fallen branch. And how sometimes, if you were quiet and lucky you could sneak up and catch turtles lying on those branches. Children would come on Saturday and Sunday mornings and go exploring or fishing. And if you stayed late into the afternoon you would hear the cicadas call and the frogs begin to croak. That creek died. A silence now replaces that which once was, never to be again.

Einige Fragen, die wir von unseren Kindern oder Enkeln niemals hören möchten, sind: "Wie konntet ihr es zulassen, dass all diese Tiere und Pflanzen ausgestorben sind? Waren sie unwichtig? Was haben sie denn falsch gemacht?"

Wir haben schon heute Ältere, die uns erzählen, wie der jetzt tote Abwasserkanal früher ein kristallklarer Bachlauf war, wo man jedes Sandkorn, selbst an den tiefsten Stellen, vom Grund her funkeln sah. Dass da Fische in den Bächen schwammen und dass Vögel sich auf abgebrochenen, darüberliegenden Ästen heranpirschten und die Fische fingen. Manchmal, wenn man sich leise an solche Zweige heran schlich und etwas Glück hatte, konnte man Schildkröten fangen, die sich auf diesen Zweigen sonnten. Kinder kamen samstags und sonntags, um zu fischen oder Neues zu entdecken. Und wenn man bis in die Abendstunden blieb, konnte man den Ruf der Zikaden und das Quaken der Frösche hören. Dieser Bach ist nun tot. Stille hat das eingenommen, was einst voller Leben war und nun für immer verloren ist.

Giant Gecko / Madagascar

Sclerosperma palm / Ghana

How do we tell the future generations what we have done, or what we have witnessed? How do we explain our failure to prevent it? How do we justify our complacency and lack of resolve? Denial is no excuse, because the signals of loss have been seen, their flames burning brightly for decades. Our generation may be recorded in history as having made the decisions that forever sacrificed the natural resources of this planet for personal comfort.

Sometimes it can be difficult to initiate change, especially if doing so requires sacrifices.

For so long we have been told that progress can be measured by increased GDP and profits and consumption, but what about quality of life? Some countries have a bill of rights to protect their citizens from all sorts of excesses, yet who legislates to ensure the newborn has the right to pure water and clean air?

Wie erklären wir kommenden Generationen, was wir getan haben oder was wir beobachtet haben? Wie erklären wir unser Versagen, diesen Verlust nicht verhindert zu haben? Wie rechtfertigen wir unsere Selbstzufriedenheit und unseren Mangel an Entschlossenheit? Es zu leugnen ist keine Entschuldigung, denn die Zeichen waren zu sehen, ihre Flammen brannten für Jahrzehnte lichterloh. Unsere Generation mag als diejenige in die Geschichte eingehen, die die natürlichen Ressourcen dieses Planeten ihrem persönlichen Komfort opferte.

Manchmal kann es schwierig sein, Änderungen anzustoßen, besonders wenn dies Opfer erfordert.

Für so lange wurde uns eingeredet, dass Fortschritt an der Steigerung von Bruttosozialprodukt, Gewinn und Verbrauch gemessen werden kann. Was aber ist mit der Lebensqualität? Einige Staaten haben Grundrechte, um ihre Bürger vor allen möglichen Arten von Ausschreitungen zu schützen, aber wo wird den Neugeborenen das Recht auf sauberes Wasser und reine Luft zugesichert?

Dypsis palm leaf

Giant gecko / Madagascar

Now is the time to take stock of the natural resources of this planet. It is imperative that we try to understand what we have before we act. Now is the time to consider what we want to leave to our children and their children's children. Now is the time to decide how we must manage these resources to maintain the richness of the existing biodiversity. And for some of the endangered plants and animals that inhabit this earth, now is our last chance.

Your future and ours are intricately linked, as we all impact on the future of this shared planet. It is up to us to make sure that our efforts produce results that nourish and preserve the earth that has for so long nourished us.

Nun ist die Zeit gekommen, eine Bestandsaufnahme der natürlichen Reserven durchzuführen. Es ist unerlässlich, dass wir versuchen zu verstehen was wir haben, bevor wir handeln. Jetzt müssen wir uns darüber klar werden, was wir unseren Kindern und Kindeskindern hinterlassen wollen. Nun geht es darum zu entscheiden, wie wir mit unseren Ressourcen umgehen müssen, um die existierende biologische Vielfalt zu erhalten. Für einige der gefährdeten Pflanzen und Tiere dieser Erde ist das jetzt die letzte Chance.

Ihre Zukunft und die unsere sind tiefgreifend miteinander verbunden, so wie wir alle die Zukunft unseres gemeinsamen Planeten beeinflussen. Es liegt nun an uns, sicherzustellen, dass unser Bemühen dazu führt, dass die Erde gehegt und bewahrt wird, wie sie uns umgekehrt schon so lange ernährt hat.

Bay of Antongil / Madagascar

Night sky in Madagascar

Acknowledgements

The Botanical Ark is a winner in 2000 of the

Slow Food International Award for Biodiversity in Food, Bologna, Italy,

and...

Jaguar/Australian Gourmet Traveller Awards of Excellence for Innovations in Tourism, Sydney, Australia

Lofty work

There are many special friends who have encouraged us, assisted us and inspired us. We wish to thank you.

Herb & Brien Bosworth
John Tan
Ian Hannaford
Michael Spyrou
Kim McDowall
Dr. Peter H. Raven
Norbert & Bettina Guthier
Terry Campbell,
Wally O'Grady
Bill Whit-man
Andreas Stoll
Joe & Billie Noli,
Gaye & Don McDowall
Mario Cobavie & Anne Quaid
Bud Quaid
Wolfgang Arnet
Kathleen Gilfedder
Donna Hedlund
Geoff Fowler & Julie Orford
Andre & Julia Leu
Mitchel & Cory Morris

Jim West & Meredith Foyle
Paul Noren & Roy Danforth
Tony Lamb
Prof. Akke Assi

Cherry Ripe
Corby Kummer
Joanna Saville
Maeve Omara
Slow Food

Bev Hill
Ian Warner
Ruth Kiew
Elizabeth Chan
Sabrina Carle
Charlotte Carle

Karin Dorn, Otto, Christine, Renate, Florian, Nette, Margo, Andreas & Dagmar Martina, Sylvia (our overseas student friends)
Douglas TAFE College Students

Rare Fruit Councils,
Heliconia Society International
And all our friends in the jungles.
And elsewhere.............

Biographies

Alan Carle was born in 1950 and spent his youth in the Catskill Mountains of New York. His parents had helped instill a deep sense of respect and wonderment for nature. Days were spent wandering the forests behind his house, and nights dreaming of the Big Island in the South Pacific - Australia.

At 19, Alan bought a one-way ticket to Australia, and emigrated to North Queensland. He arrived with 80 cents . His dream was to study and live on the Great Barrier Reef. During his time at University Alan realised that Queensland had a Government that wanted to drill for oil on the Great Barrier Reef and chop down the rainforests for woodchips. He began working for the regional Conservation Council and actively worked on campaigns that helped prevent that destruction and preserve some of the areas that are a unique part of North Queensland's natural and Aboriginal heritage.

Susan arrived in 1975 and stayed. In 1977 they decided to raise a family in a way that was sensitive to nature and sustainable.

Alan Carle, Jahrgang 1950, verbrachte seine Jugend in den Catskill-Mountains im US-Bundesstaat New York. Seine Eltern vermittelten ihm hohen Respekt für die Natur und sorgten auch dafür, dass er das Staunen über sie nicht verlernte. Tags streifte er durch die Wälder hinter dem Haus und nachts träumte er von der großen Insel im Südpazifik - Australien.

Mit 19 kaufte sich Alan ein Oneway-Ticket nach Australien und wanderte nach Nord-Queensland aus. Er kam dort mit 80 Cents an. Sein Traum war es, am Great Barrier Reef zu wohnen und es zu studieren. Während seiner Zeit an der Universität erkannte Alan, dass die Regierung von Queensland im Riff nach Öl bohren und den Regenwald abholzen wollte, um ihn zu Holzspänen zu verarbeiten. Er begann, für den örtlichen Umweltschutz zu arbeiten und beteiligte sich aktiv an Kampagnen, die halfen, diese Zerstörung zu verhindern. Sie retteten auch einige der Gebiete, die zum einzigartigen Naturerbe von Nord-Queensland und der Aborigines gehören.

Susan besuchte Alan 1975 und blieb. 1977 beschlossen die beiden, eine Familie zu gründen, die sich einfühlsam und dauerhaft an den Belangen der Natur orientierte.

Susan (Hedlund) Carle was born in 1956 in New York. She spent her childhood at the Norwegian's Children's Home in Bay Ridge, Brooklyn, and every summer went to camp in the Catskill Mountains.

When Susan was 10 years old she met Alan, who was always talking of Australia. In 1975 after finishing school and studying at Brooklyn College and Ulster College, she went to Australia to visit Alan . Twenty-six years later she is still here. Susan is now a dual citizen.

In 1984 Susan discovered her 'lost' family in New York and Northern Sweden.

Susan gave birth to their daughter Heather on their first 'fruitful' exploring trip through the Pacific, Central and South America and Florida in 1978. Cali was born in Australia in 1980 and Susan began to create the home and look after the flower business and garden.

Now that the girls are grown up Susan again accompanies Alan on trips into the remaining rainforests.

Susan (Hedlund) Carle wurde 1956 in New York geboren. Sie verbrachte ihre Kindheit in einem norwegischen Kinderheim in Bay Ridge, Brooklyn. Jeden Sommer ging sie zum Zelten in die Catskill Mountains.

Susan & Alan Carle

Mit 10 Jahren traf Susan Alan zum ersten Mal. Der redete immer nur über eines - Australien. 1975, nach ihrem Schul- und Studienabschluss am Brooklyn- und Ulster-College, besuchte sie Alan in Australien. Sechsundzwanzig Jahre später ist sie immer noch dort. Susan hat jetzt die doppelte Staatsbürgerschaft.

1984 entdeckte Susan ihre "verlorene" Familie in New York und Nordschweden. 1978, in Florida, bekam Susan ihre erste Tochte, Heather. Das war während ihrer ersten "fruchtbaren Entdeckungsreise" durch den Pazifik, Mittel- und Südamerika. Cali, die zweite Tochter, wurde 1980 in Australien geboren. Susan begann, das Haus einzurichten und sich um das Blumengeschäft und den Garten zu kümmern. Nun, da die Töchter erwachsen sind, begleitet Susan Alan wieder auf seinen Exkursionen durch die noch verbliebenen Regenwälder.

Norbert Guthier was born in 1954 in Heppenheim, Germany. Since completing his photography studies in 1982, he has worked as a freelance photo designer in Frankfurt. He has become well-known for his numerous international exhibitions and books on the topic of nude photography.

What only a few people know, however, is that Norbert Guthier's second greatest passion is for the remaining rain forests in the world. Outfitted with his cameras, he loves to dive deep into the fascinating world of the tropics. In addition to his photographic interests of capturing and preserving the unparalleled atmosphere of the rain forest in pictures, he also wishes to contribute to the preservation of these endangered paradises. Norbert Guthier met Alan in 1997 while on a photo journey in Australia, and was so impressed by his work and commitment, that in the following year he accompanied Alan on a trip to the Ivory Coast, Cameroon and Ghana in order to document Alan's work photographically.

It was during a joint expedition in Madagascar in autumn 2000 that the idea arose to put this book together, which they began to design the following spring when Norbert visited the Botanical Ark for four weeks. A further book about the rain forest with stereo and panorama photographs is in the works.

Norbert Guthier

Norbert Guthier wurde 1954 in Heppemheim, Deutschland geboren. Seit dem Abschluß seines Fotodesignstudiums 1982 arbeitet er als freischaffender Fotodesigner in Frankfurt. Bekannt wurde er durch zahlreiche internationale Ausstellungen und Bücher zum Thema Aktfotografie.

Was aber nur wenige wissen: Norbert Guthiers zweite große Leidenschaft gilt den noch verbliebenen Regenwäldern dieser Welt. Ausgerüstet mit der Fotokamera liebt er es, in die faszinierende Welt der Tropen abzutauchen. Neben seinem fotografischen Interesse, die einzigartige Stimmung der Regenwälder in Bildern festzuhalten, möchte er mit seiner Arbeit auch zum Erhalt dieser bedrohten Paradiese beitragen. Er lernte Alan 1997 anläßlich einer Fotoreise nach Australien kennen und war von dessen Arbeit und Engagement so begeistert, daß er ihn im darauf folgenden Jahr auf seinen Reisen an die Cote d'Ivoire, nach Kamerun und Ghana begleitete, um Alan's Arbeit fotografisch zu dokumentieren.

Bei einer gemeinsamen Expedition im Herbst 2000 auf Madagaskar entstand die Idee zu dem vorliegenden Buch, das im folgenden Frühjahr bei einem vierwöchigen Aufenthalt auf der Botanical Ark Gestalt annahm. Ein weiteres Buch zum Thema Regenwald mit Stereo- und Panorama-Aufnahmen ist in Arbeit.

Thanks To

If it wasn't for the support of various companies and individuals, this book wouldn't have become a reality. They feel called - just as the authors Alan Carle and Norbert Guthier - to support the preservation of nature, to lead the way and not hope for others to take the initiative. Our thanks go especially to:

Firmen und Einzelpersonen haben die Realisation dieses Buches erst ermöglicht. Sie fühlten sich - ganz im Sinne der Autoren Alan Carle und Norbert Guthier - aufgefordert, das Engagement für den Erhalt unserer Natur zu unterstützen, voranzugehen und nicht auf die Initiative anderer zu hoffen. Unser Dank gilt im Besonderen:

Nestlé Erzeugnisse Frankfurt / Germany

Handelspresse Offenbach / Germany

Gerasch & Company Communication Darmstadt / Germany

Tropica Raritäten Gärtnerei Kriftel / Germany

hair.style.Paul Mitchell Malchen / Germany

Papier Union Flörsheim / Germany

Bühler & Partners Frankfurt / Germany

The Botanical Ark has not been designed for the mass tourism market and is **not open** to the general public. This is the Carle's personal home. It is only open to special groups (12 or more) (or at a group rate) - and only by prior arrangements.

Die Botanical Ark ist das Privatanwesen der Familie Carle. Sie ist nicht für den Massentourismus ausgelegt und daher auch der Öffentlichkeit **nicht** zugänglich. Nur nach vorheriger Absprache können gebuchte Gruppen von 12 oder mehr Personen die Botanical Ark besuchen.

text: Alan & Susan Carle
photos: Norbert Guthier
preface: Dr. Peter H. Raven

address: Alan & Susan Carle
PO Box 354
Mossman 4873, Queensland / Australia
internet: www.botanicalark.com
e-mail: info@botanicalark.com
phone: +61 740 988174
fax: +61 740 988173

address: Norbert Guthier
Westerbachstr.105
D 65936 Frankfurt / Germany
internet: www.guthier.info
www.guthier.com
e-mail: info@guthier.com
phone: + 49 69 345757
fax: + 49 69 345900

the german library: Die Deutsche Bibliothek
CIP-Cataloguing-in-Publication-Data
A catalogue record for this publication is available from Die Deutsche Bibilothek.

first edition: 2002
printed in: Germany
publisher: Norbert Guthier, Frankfurt
printing: Druckhaus Neppe, Hainburg
binding: C. Fikentscher, Darmstadt
paper: Printed on Galaxi 150 GSM, Wood-free, Non-chlorine bleached, White photo stock with ceramic finish from Paper Union
translation: Werner & Karen Steuer, Darmstadt

isbn no.: 3-00-008660-9